P9-CRZ-266

Big Idea's VeggieTales Bible Storybook

With Scripture from the NIrV

This book belongs to:

_____

BIG IDEA BOOKS

ZONDERk·dz

Sunday Morning Values, Saturday Morning Fun®
Now That's a Big Idea!

ZONDERVAN.com/
AUTHORTRACKER
follow your favorite authors

www.bigidea.com

The VeggieTales® Bible Storybook
Copyright © 2006 by Big Idea, Inc.
Illustration copyright © 2006 by Big Idea, Inc.

Requests for information should be addressed to:
Zonderkidz, Grand Rapids, MI 49530

Library of Congress Cataloging-in-Publication Data

Kenney, Cindy, 1959-
   VeggieTales Bible storybook : with Scripture from the NIrV / by
Cindy Kenney with Karen Poth.
      p. cm.
   ISBN-13: 978-0-310-71008-0 (printed hardcover)
   ISBN-10: 0-310-71008-1 (printed hardcover)
   1. Bible stories, English.   I. Poth, Karen 1966-   II. Title.
BS551.3.K46 2006
220.9'505—dc22

2006007373

All Scripture quotations, unless otherwise indicated, are taken from the
HOLY BIBLE, NEW INTERNATIONAL READER'S VERSION®. Copyright
© 1995, 1996, 1998 by International Bible Society. Used by permission
of Zondervan. All Rights Reserved.

All rights reserved. No part of this publication may be reproduced, stored in
a retrieval system, or transmitted in any form or by any means—electronic,
mechanical, photocopy, recording, or any other—except for brief quotations
in printed reviews, without the prior permission of the publisher.

Big Idea is a registered trademark of Big Idea, Inc.

Zonderkidz is a trademark of Zondervan.

Editor: Catherine DeVries
Art Direction and Design: Karen Poth and Ron Eddy
Production Artist: Sarah Jongsma
Written by: Cindy Kenney with Karen Poth
Illustrated by: Casey Jones and Robert Vann

Printed in USA
08 09 10 11 12 13 • 13 12 11 10 9 8

Table of Contents

Unless otherwise specified below, all story titles are from VeggieTales videos of the same name.

1. From Duke and the Great Pie War
2. Based on book of same title
3. From Where's God When I'm S-Scared?
4. From Jonah, A VeggieTales® Movie
5. Based on book of same title
6. From Are You My Neighbor?
7. From God Wants Me to Forgive Them!?!
8. From Are You My Neighbor?

Howdy partners!

Some folks have been teasin' and pushin' my partner, Bob the Tomato, around lately. The other day, somebody filled his mailbox with whipped cream. I thought he should sprinkle in some nuts ... add a little hot fudge ... a cherry ... and enjoy the treat!

Bob disagreed. And he really got his feelings hurt too because it's hard when things always seem to be going wrong. So I found a rootin' tootin' western Bible story that had all the fixin's to help Bob solve his problem!

The Ballad of Little Joe

Yippee ki
yay ki yay!
Today is a
special day!

Way out west, at the Okie Dokie
Corral, lived a guy named Little Joe. He
lived with his eleven cowboy brothers, all
of whom had French accents.

Little Joe was his father's favorite son.
So for his birthday, his dad gave him
a beautiful western vest
of many colors. Now, his
brothers didn't like that
one bit.

6

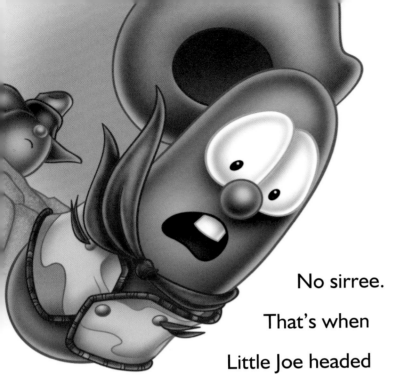

You were always Pa's favorite son.

No sirree. That's when Little Joe headed into all sorts of trouble! His brothers were so jealous, they decided to toss him right into an old mine shaft!

"Hey, Jude!" Little Joe called out to his big brother for help.

But Jude didn't answer. Instead, he convinced the rest of his brothers to hand Little Joe over to a band of desperados.

The desperados sold Little Joe to the owner of the Rootin' Tootin' Pizza Place in Dodge Ball City. But Little Joe made the best of the situation. He worked so hard that he was named employee of the month! Unfortunately, that made Miss Kitty, the waitress at the Rootin' Tootin' Pizza Place, burning mad. Miss Kitty decided to get even with Little Joe. She filled his cow hat with lots of money and told everybody Little Joe had stolen it!

My belief that God is good helps overcome frustration.

The sheriff rounded up Little Joe and tossed him in jail. Once again he found himself in a whole lick of trouble!

"Little Joe, why is all this stuff happening to you?" asked Sheriff Bob.

"Shucks! I don't really know. But God is good," Little Joe answered. "I reckon I just have to keep on doin' what's right."

so I'll keep doin' what is right, despite incarceration.

9

You're not still upset about that little mine shaft joke, are you?

One night, the mayor of Dodge Ball City had a dream. He was so upset by it, he simply had to know what it meant.

Little Joe asked God to help him explain the mayor's dream.

Little Joe told the mayor he would have seven years of more food than they knew what to do with and seven years of terrible famine.

The mayor was so impressed, he made Little Joe the second most powerful man in Dodge Ball City. And Little Joe used his new position to get the town ready for the seven bad years.

During those bad years, Little Joe's

family came to Dodge Ball City. They were hungry and they needed some food.

At first, Little Joe was mad at them. But he knew God had used all the bad things that had happened to him for good. So he forgave his brothers, and they had the best family reunion the west had ever seen! **End**

The Bible Story

Yee-ha! I sure am glad God's in charge. We can always count on God when times are bad. And that should keep us from being sad. Read all about it in the story of Joseph.

The story of Joseph

selections from Genesis 37:1–45:8

Israel loved Joseph more than any of his other sons [and] made him a beautiful robe. Joseph's brothers saw that their father loved him more than any of them. They hated Joseph [and] threw him into [an empty] well. Then they [sold] him to some traders. The traders took him to Egypt ... and sold Joseph to Potiphar, one of Pharaoh's officials. He was the captain of the palace guard.

Potiphar's wife [lied about Joseph] and so Potiphar ... put Joseph in prison.

[A few years later, Pharaoh sent for Joseph] and said, "I had a dream. No one can tell me what it means. But I've heard that when you hear a dream you can explain it." Joseph said, "God has shown Pharaoh what he's about to do. Seven years with plenty of food are coming to the whole land of Egypt. But seven years when there won't be enough food will follow them. The grain should be stored up for the country to use later."

Pharaoh put Joseph in charge of the whole land.

God sent me ahead of you to save many lives.

Joseph's brothers went to buy grain there. Joseph recognized his brothers, but they didn't recognize him. Joseph said, "Come close to me. I am your brother Joseph. I'm the one you sold into Egypt. But don't be upset. And don't be angry with yourselves because you sold me here. God sent me ahead of you to save many lives."

So kids,

Have you ever had to deal with some double trouble in your life? Or maybe you've just been doggone sad about something?

By golly, when Bob heard about how Little Joe trusted God to make good out of the bad things that happened to him, he felt a lot better!

It sure is nice to know that God's got a plan—and he can turn bad things into something good!

That's because...
God made you special and he loves you very much!

14

Hi everybody!

Do you know someone who's always the center of attention? Like a younger brother or sister who needs to be cared for—all the time? Well that's my little brother, Lenny.

Today Lenny made us all watch as he jumped HEAD FIRST into the pool. Then, when he lost his propeller hat, I had to stop swimming and take care of him!

Later, Bob found me pouting as I floated down the lazy river in the water park. That's when he told me the story of Miriam, and I realized I was heading the wrong way ...

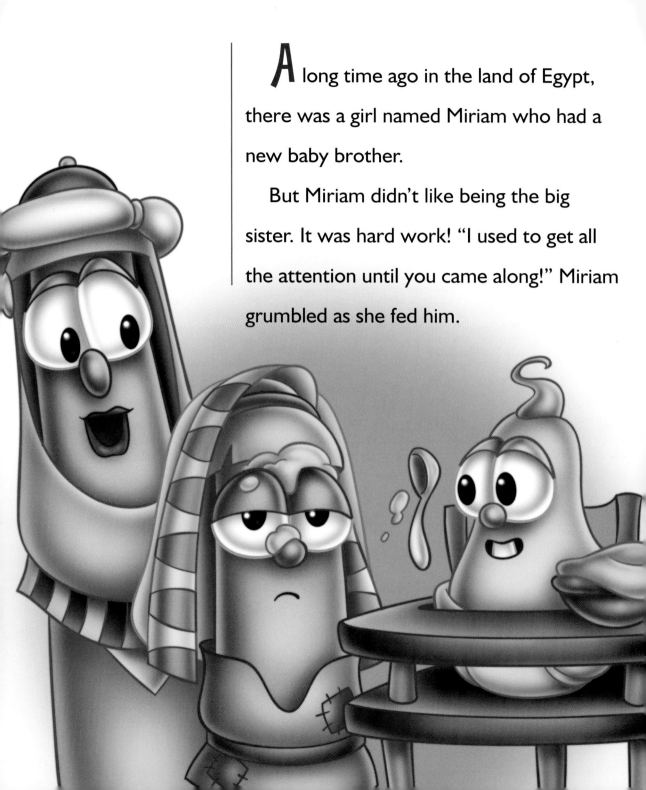

A long time ago in the land of Egypt, there was a girl named Miriam who had a new baby brother.

But Miriam didn't like being the big sister. It was hard work! "I used to get all the attention until you came along!" Miriam grumbled as she fed him.

But no one paid attention to Miriam. They were all worried about a new law that might put their newest family member in great danger.

The king of Egypt didn't want any more baby boys living in his kingdom. He was worried that some day they might grow up and fight against him. So the king's guards were told to take all the baby boys away from their families. Miriam's little brother had to be protected from the guards.

"Now you're the big sister," Miriam's mother told her. "And being part of a family means taking care of each other."

I can't have fun, because of all that must be done!

There's
something
suspicious
going
on here.

Every day Miriam took
care of her brother while her mother and
father worked for the king. The guards
spied on them, to see if the baby was a boy.

So Miriam was very careful to protect
him. When the guards peeked in the
windows or sneaked in the door, Miriam
held up a stinky diaper to scare them.

"Peeea-u!" they shouted and ran away.

"I sure liked it better when I was the baby," Miriam grumbled, again.

One day, Miriam was crossing the street when a royal carriage came racing around the corner. She would have been hit, but her big brother Aaron leaped into the street and saved her.

Suddenly Miriam realized what it meant to be a part of the family. And she knew she needed a better plan to protect her little brother.

So, how do you, like, take care of one of these things?

Miriam knew that the princess liked to swim in the river. So Miriam put her little brother in a basket and floated him down the Nile. Hiding among the weeds, Miriam waited as the basket floated right into the princess' arms!

"Wow! What a cute baby!" the princess exclaimed.

But the princess didn't know how to

take care of a baby. So Miriam offered to be his babysitter. The princess agreed and told the guards to leave Miriam and the baby alone. Miriam took Moses safely back home. Miriam's mother was so proud of her because she put her brother's needs before her own! **End**

So you're, like, a babysitter?

The Bible Story

Do your mom and dad ever ask you to do things you don't want to? God wants us to remember that being part of a family means putting their needs first. You can read about Miriam's story in the Bible.

Miriam's Story
selections from Exodus 1:22– 2:10

[A slave woman] became pregnant and had a son. She saw that her baby was a fine child. So she hid him for three months. After that, she couldn't hide him any longer. So she got a basket that was made out of the stems of tall grass. She coated it with tar. Then she placed the child in it. She put the basket in the tall grass that grew along the bank of the Nile River.

The child's sister [Miriam] wasn't very far away. She wanted to see what would happen to him. Pharaoh's daughter went down to the Nile River to take a bath. She saw the basket in the tall grass. So she sent her slave to get it. When she opened it, she saw the baby. He was crying. She felt sorry for him. "This is one of the Hebrew babies," she said.

Then [Miriam] spoke to Pharaoh's daughter. She asked, "Do you want me to go and get one of the Hebrew women? She could nurse the baby for you."

"Yes. Go," she answered. So the girl went and got the baby's mother.

She named him Moses... "I pulled him out of the water."

Pharaoh's daughter said to her, "Take this baby. Nurse him for me. I'll pay you."

When the child grew older, [his mother] took him [back to] Pharaoh's daughter. And he became her son. She named him Moses. She said, "I pulled him out of the water."

Bob was right.

I was heading the wrong way—but not down the lazy river! I was heading the wrong direction in my thinking. I was thinking a lot more about myself than my little brother.

God wants us to put others first—even our baby brothers and sisters. That's the best way we can show our love. God shows us how much he loves us every day. His love is always flowing like a river—a river flowing exactly the right way. I can show how much I love him by putting other's needs before my own.

Let's all do something special for someone today.

Remember...
God made you special and he loves you very much!

Anyone who loves God must also love his brothers and sisters.

— I John 4:21

Hi kids!

According to Larry's calculations, he has invited Cornelius Corn and Barbara Beet to Sunday school nearly six zillion, five thousand and two times. Then he invited them to come see a VeggieTales show with him three thousand, four hundred and seven times. Their answer was always the same—no.

Larry was hoping to tell his friends about God, but he's getting tired of trying. He's tired of counting, too. That's when I told him it was time for war—Frog Wars.

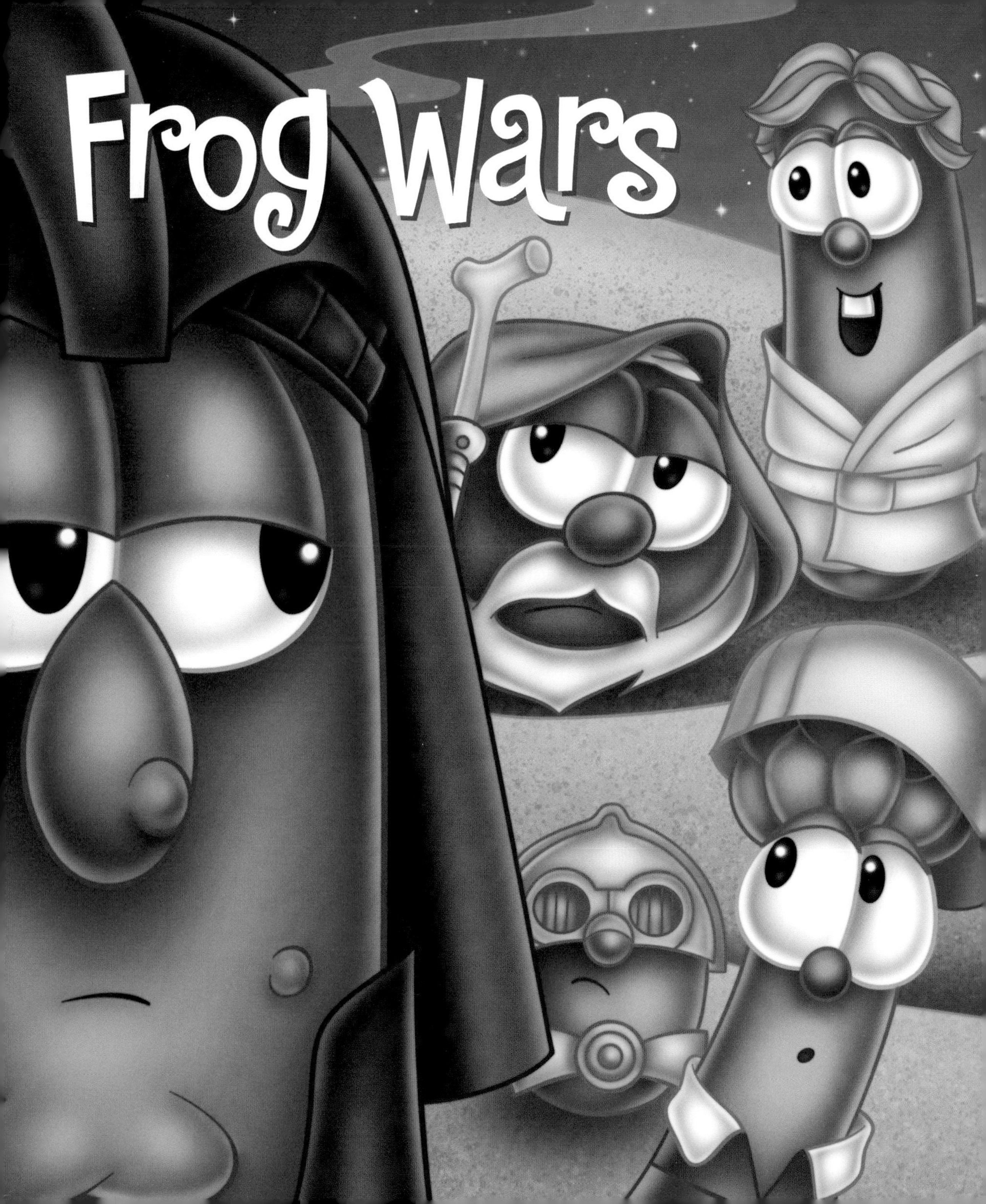
Frog Wars

Junior was greeted by Cuke Sandwalker, Princess Hair-Spraya,

A long time ago, on a countertop far, far away, Junior Asparagus found himself standing beside a mysterious statue of a frog. Suddenly Cuke Sandwalker and Princess Hair-Spraya approached Junior and asked if he was sent by God to set them and the thousands of slaves free from Dark Visor's reign. A bit confused, Junior was led into a giant throne room to see Dark Visor.

Junior was very nervous as he stood before the king. After some persuading, he finally squeaked out something about letting the slaves go free.

"NO!" came the thundering voice of the king. Then his visor slammed shut.

"Okay, I tried," Junior shrugged. "Trying isn't really my thing."

"Then stick with me!" a big tomato said as he came into the room with his walking stick. "We won't give up until Dark Visor gives in!"

"My name is Mo! And God wants you to let his people go!" the tomato demanded of Dark Visor.

and two peas called Sweet-Pea-3-Oh and Achoo Bless-U.

God caused swarms of dust bunnies, a drought of pizza and ice cream, and days and days of the Hokey Pokey!

"Whmmmimmtwy-outtodsiiiiiiii!" Dark Visor shouted back, forgetting to lift his visor before speaking.

Dark Visor would not let the slaves go free. But did Mo give up? Nope! He put his faith in God.

God caused many plagues to come upon the land to convince Dark Visor to let the slaves go free.

The water turned into grape juice.

And there was an invasion of frogs!

Junior didn't want to hang in there anymore. But he knew that God wants us to put our hope in him and keep trying.

Then God sent a deep darkness that finally caused Dark Visor to let the slaves go free!

"Hurray!" everyone shouted as they marched out of the land. Junior rode in a wagon with his new friends.

There wasn't any room for Cuke in the wagon. "Use the horse, Cuke!"

Junior was scared, but he didn't give up!

Suddenly, Dark Visor yelled, "Ichkabild Goafrtthslvsflnan!"

"He changed his mind!" the guards shouted. "Go after them!"

The Empire was striking back!

The slaves were trapped in front of the Big Frog Pond as the king's army caught up to them. But did Junior give up? Nope! He had hope.

God made the lily pads come together as stepping stones over the waters, so everyone could get to the other side.

As Dark Visor's army followed behind, the lily pads returned to normal, and the guards sank into the mud and water.

The slaves cheered! Because they had trusted God and not given up, God showed them a way to escape.

From then on, Junior knew how important it was to never give up! **End**

He knew they had to trust God in a mighty way.

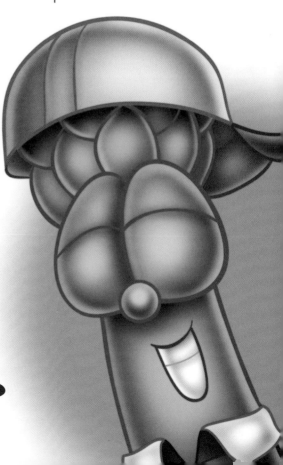

The Bible Story

Wow! I sure did learn how important it is to try hard and not give up! God helped Moses to keep on going over and over again in the book of Exodus.

The Story of Moses

selections from Exodus 3–14

The LORD said [to Moses], "I have seen my people suffer in Egypt. I have heard them cry out ... So now, go. I am sending you to Pharaoh. I want you to bring the Israelites out of Egypt ... I will strike the Egyptians with all kinds of miracles (river turning to blood, frogs, gnats, flies, boils, darkness, and more). After that, [Pharaoh] will let you go." Moses did all of those miracles in the sight of Pharaoh. [Finally] ... Pharaoh said to them, "Get out of here! You and the Israelites, leave my people! Go."

Then Pharaoh and his officials changed their minds. They said, "What have we done? We've lost our slaves and all of the work they used to do for us!"

The LORD spoke to Moses. He said, "... Hold your wooden staff out. Reach your hand out over the Red Sea to part the water. Then the people can go through the sea on dry ground." The people of Israel went through the sea on dry ground. There was a wall of water on their right side and on their left.

The Egyptians chased them [in over 600 chariots]. Then the LORD [told] Moses, "Reach your hand out over the sea." The water flowed back. It covered the entire army of Pharaoh that had followed the people of Israel into the sea. Not one of the Egyptians was left.

The people of Israel went through the sea on dry ground.

So you see kids,

Larry and I both learned a lot from that lesson. It's always easier to give up on something than it is to keep trying.

Larry didn't stop inviting Cornelius Corn and Barbara Beet to church. And Cornelius finally went with us last week!

God just wants us to remember to do our best. That's all any of us can do. Next time you feel like giving up, just think about what God wants you to do and keep trying! Remember, God is on your side.

Because...
God made you special and he loves you very much!

Be strong, all you who ... hope in the LORD. Never give up.

— Psalm 31:24

Hi guys!

Do you ever wonder why you have to go to bed so early? Why you have to pick up ALL your toys? Or why you HAVE to clean your plate when you go to Aunt Ruth's house for dinner—even if it's liver?

Sometimes I think rules are just plain silly.

But then Larry told me that there were a whole lot of people in the Bible who thought rules were silly, too. He told me the story of Josh and the Big Wall!

We didn't have a lot of fun in the desert. We didn't have a lot of fun in the sand.

Remember how God helped the slaves escape Egypt? He had a special place for them to go called the promised land.

But, unfortunately, as they got closer to the promised land, the Israelites started doing things THEIR way and ignoring God's rules. When that happened, things got a little goofy. So God let them wander in the desert for a little while—about forty years!

When God decided the Israelites were
ready to go into their new land, he chose
Joshua to be their leader. Off they went,
until BUMMMMP! They bonked right into
a huge wall blocking the land called Jericho.

Two French peas were standing guard
on the wall. "Who are you?" they asked.

"I am Joshua. And these are the children
of Israel. God has given us this land for our
new home. So you're, um, going to have
to leave."

I've got slushee in my ear!

The French peas just laughed. "Go away, you tiny pickle," they said to Joshua.

One of the soldiers laughed so hard he knocked a cup full of slushee right on their heads.

Joshua decided to ask God what to do. The answer he got wasn't something the Israelites expected.

God told Joshua to have the Israelites march around the city every day for seven days. Jimmy and Jerry Gourd thought that was crazy! So they came up with their own way to bring down the walls of Jericho—the Walminator 3000!

That's when Junior Asparagus stood up and said, "God gave us directions, and we're ignoring them! Things always work out better when we do things God's way instead of our way!"

Blowin' horns in the desert isn't gonna do it.

The LORD has given this land to us ...

So the next seven days, the Israelites marched around the walls of Jericho—even when the pea guards dropped slushees on them!

The Israelites followed God's plan and did exactly what God said. On the seventh day, they marched around Jericho seven times while the priests blew their horns. With one final trumpet blast, the people shouted and there was a great RUMMMBLING!

We know
that he will
take care of
us, if we will
follow him.

The walls fell down, just as God had promised! Now the Israelites could enter the promised land!

"You see?" Joshua explained. "Sometimes God asks us to do things that don't make sense to us. But when we remember that God loves us and wants what's best for us, we can be sure that his way is the best way." End

The Bible Story

Sometimes it's hard to understand all the rules God wants us to obey. But God wants us to obey him, because he loves us so much! He shows us that over and over! You can read about it in the Bible.

The Battle of Jericho

selections from Joshua 5:13–6:27

The gates of Jericho were shut tight and guarded closely. No one went out. No one came in.

The LORD spoke to Joshua. He said, "I have handed Jericho over to you. I have also handed its king and its fighting men over to you. March around the city once with all of your fighting men. In fact, do it for six days. Have seven priests get trumpets that are made out of rams' horns. They must carry them in front of the ark of the covenant. On the seventh day, march around the city seven times. Have the priests blow the trumpets as you march. You will hear them blow a long blast on the trumpets. When you do, have all of the men give a loud shout. The wall of the city will fall down. Then the whole army will go up to the city. Every man will go straight in."

So Joshua ... gave an order to the men. He said, "Move out! March

> Have all of the men give a loud shout. The wall of the city will fall down.

around the city." On the seventh day, they got up at sunrise. They marched around the city, just as they had done before. But on that day they went around it seven times. On the seventh time around, the priests blew a long blast on the trumpets. Then Joshua gave a command to the men. He said, "Shout! The LORD has given you the city!"

Guess what?

I sure do feel more like obeying the rules now. God makes rules because he loves us. He gave me parents to take care of me. And they make rules because they love me, too.

So I guess I better pick up my toys. My mom and dad probably give me a bedtime so I don't get tired and sick. And I'll clean my plate when I go to Aunt Ruth's house—even if it's liver!!

Have you ever felt a rule was silly? Ask a grown-up you trust to explain it to you. There's probably a good reason for it.

And remember...
God made you special and he loves you very much!

If you obey my commands, you will remain in my love.

— John 15:10

51

Hi kids!

The other day I had a real problem. There's a new boy at school named Ulf. And he was looking for a place to sit at lunch. As he walked by my table, I was about to ask him if he wanted to sit down, because I know that's what God would want me to do. But I was afraid the Zucchini brothers would be mad at me if I did. They say that Ulf eats strange food.

I asked Bob and he told me I should read the story of Gideon—Tuba Warrior.

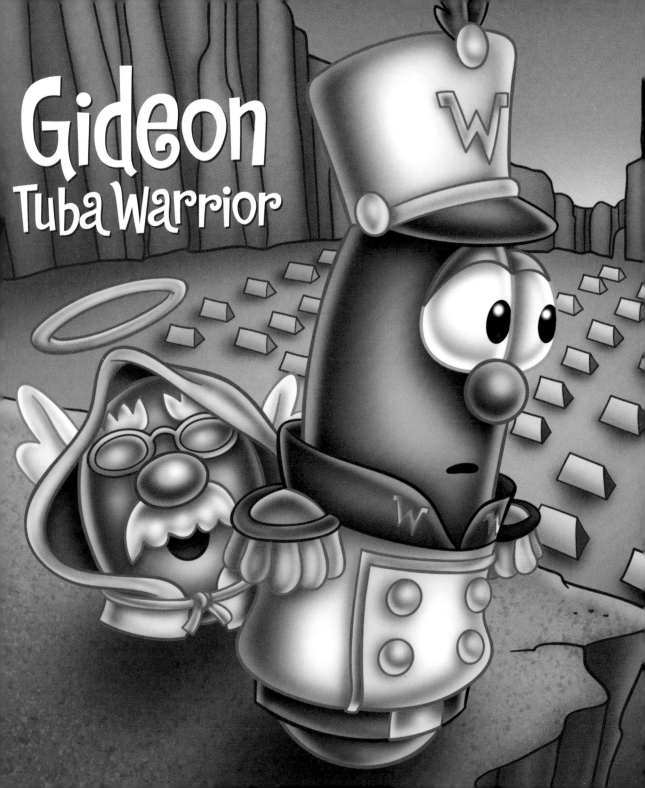

One sunny afternoon Gideon was in his backyard practicing his tuba when suddenly an angel appeared. "Greetings, human. I'm an angel."

"The Angels, huh?" Gideon replied, "I'm a Warrior. Do we play your team this year?"

"No, no, no," the angel said. "I'm a REAL angel sent to you from the Lord above with a message."

54

"So Mr. Angel," Gideon said, "what's your message?"

"Here's the skinny," the angel replied. "You have been chosen to lead Israel's army against a ferocious enemy."

Gideon was sure the angel was making a mistake. He explained to the angel that he was a tuba player, not a warrior. But the angel assured him that he was the one chosen by God to fight an army of huge, hairy Midianites.

I've got
to know
absolutely,
that God
is in this.

Gideon just could not believe that God wanted him. He asked for a sign from God. So that night, Gideon laid a piece of fleece down on the ground. In the morning, if the fleece was wet and the ground was dry around it, then he would believe that this was God's will. The next morning Gideon checked the fleece. Sure enough, the ground around the fleece was dry, but the fleece was soaking wet. "God has chosen ME!"

Now the hard work would begin. Gideon had to gather an army.

"Join God's army and get a free flashlight," he yelled as soldiers flocked to their new leader. Just as Gideon was beginning to feel confident with the size of his army, the angel pulled him aside.

"There are too many," he said. "You have to get rid of some of them."

Gideon couldn't believe it, but he did as the angel ordered and sent half his army home.

Send soldiers home? You have got to be kidding!

God's our friend through thick and thin.

On the day of the battle, Gideon got very nervous about his small army.

"Do you ever have any trouble trusting God?" Gideon asked the angel.

"Me? No, I see him every day!" the angel told him. "Trust him, Gideon. He'll never let you down."

So Gideon prayed to God. "You and I both know I can't do this on my own," he said, "but you can, and that's good enough for me."

Even though they were out-numbered by more than three-thousand-to-one, Gideon's small army of marching band warriors defeated the Midianites that night ... using only their horns and their flashlights!

"God chose me for this time and this place," Gideon told his troops. "All I did was trust that he would do what he said. And he did." End

The Bible Story

And there you have it. Gideon was the most courageous Tuba Warrior in history. He trusted God no matter what. If we all trust God no matter what, we will be victorious, too!

Gideon's Story

selections from Judges 6:35–7:22

Gideon said to God, "You promised you would use me to save Israel. I'll put a piece of wool on the threshing floor. Suppose dew is only on the wool tomorrow morning. And suppose the ground all around it is dry. Then I will know that you will use me to save Israel. I'll know that your promise will come true." Gideon got up early the next day. He squeezed the dew out of the wool. Then Gideon said to God, "Don't let your anger burn against me. Let me ask you for just one more thing. Let me use the wool for one more test. This time make the wool dry. And cover the ground with dew." So that night God did it.

The LORD spoke to Gideon. He said, "I want to hand Midian over to you. But you have too many men for me to do that. I do not want Israel to brag that their own strength has saved them. So Gideon took 300 men. During that night the LORD spoke to Gideon. He said, "Get up. Go down against the camp. I am going to hand it over to you. Gideon separated the 300 men into three companies. He put a trumpet and an empty jar into the hands of each man. And he put a torch inside each jar. "Watch me," he told them. "Do what I do. I'll go to the edge of the enemy camp. Then do exactly as I do. I and everyone who is with me will blow our trumpets. Then blow your trumpets from your positions all around the camp. And shout the battle cry, 'For the LORD and for Gideon!' " The LORD caused all of the men in the enemy camp to start fighting each other. They attacked each other with their swords. Gideon … [destroyed their whole army].

I know that your promise will come true.

Well, what do ya know?

I guess I should show kindness to Ulf and ask him to sit at my table. Being kind to everyone is something that God asks all of us to do. Even if they eat strange food. And just like Gideon, I have to trust that if I do what God asks me to do I will be a winner every time.

If the Zucchini brothers don't like it when I do the right thing, then I can trust God to help me find new friends who will.

Remember...
God made you special and he loves you very much!

Trust in the Lord with all your heart. Do not depend on your own understanding.

— Proverbs 3:5

Hi there!

Have you ever felt like you wanted to do something but couldn't? When I was little, I always wanted to be able to play the harmonica while riding a skateboard down a big hill ... just like my older cousin, Hank. He was really great at it. And he told me I was too little to do it right.

I would get so frustrated. But Bob made me feel better one day. He told me not to give up, and he suggested that I read the story of Dave and the Giant Pickle.

Oh, Dave! One of my sheep fell over!

Once there was a small shepherd boy named Dave who had seven brothers. They lived in Israel and spent their time in the field taking care of sheep—sheep that tipped over!

Dave's father had to send his brothers to help fight the Philistines—the people who hated Israel. But Dave couldn't go because he was just a little guy.

Why can't little guys do big things, too?

Dave wondered.

Fighting the Philistines wasn't easy! They made a crummy deal with the Israelites. Both armies had to send their biggest and strongest man out to fight each other. Whoever lost the battle would have to be the slaves of the other country.

Why can't little guys do big things, too?

After we defeat you, you will have to fetch our slippers and wipe our little noses!

Suddenly the land began to tremble! Boom! Boom! BOOM! A giant pickle named Goliath appeared and asked, "Who will I fight?"

The Israelites were terrified of Goliath. They ran away and hid!

"I'll come back tomorrow," said the pickle. He came back again, and again! For forty days the Israelites ran away and hid.

David's dad was worried about his boys. So he sent little Dave to the battlefield with pizza for his brothers.

Dave was surprised that no one would fight Goliath.

"C'mon guys! We're the children of God!" Dave reminded everyone.

But the Israelites were too
scared. They had forgotten
that God was much bigger
than any giant! So little Dave
agreed to fight him.

I will
fight
you,
Goliath!

"That's a job for a big person, not a little boy like you!" said King Saul.

"You're big," said Dave. "I'm little. My head only comes to your middle. But little guys can do big things, too!"

Dave trusted God, so he faced the giant pickle all alone.

"Who will fight me?" the giant asked.

"I come before you in the name of the God of Israel who will help me defeat you!" Dave said.

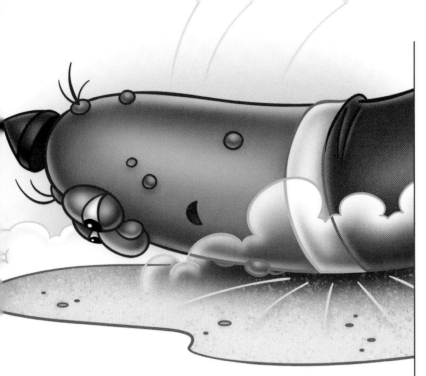

Everyone watched as the giant wiggled a little, then wobbled a little, then fell flat on his face!

Then he bravely put a stone into his slingshot and let it fly. The stone struck Goliath right on his noggin.

Goliath fell down ... down ... DOWN to the ground.

"Hurray!" the Israelites shouted. They were saved!

And that's the story of Dave—a really little guy who did a really big thing! End

The Bible Story

It was really scary facing a giant pickle! But I trusted God, because he made each of us very special. You can read about the real story of David and Goliath in the Bible.

David and Goliath
selections from 1 Samuel 17:1-58

The Philistine army was camped on one hill. Israel's army was on another. The valley was between them. Jesse's three oldest sons had followed Saul into battle. David was the youngest. He [took] care of his father's sheep.

Early [one] morning David loaded up food and [went to give it to his brothers]. As they were [eating], Goliath stepped forward from his line. Goliath was a mighty Philistine hero. He was more than nine feet tall. He again dared someone to fight him.

David said to King Saul, "Don't let anyone lose hope because of that Philistine. I'll go out and fight him." Saul replied, "You aren't able to go out there and fight that Philistine. You are too young. He's been a fighting man ever since he was a boy."

David said, "The LORD saved me from the paw of the lion. He saved me from the paw of the bear. And he'll save me from the powerful hand of this Philistine too."

David went down to a stream and chose five smooth stones. He said, "Goliath, you are coming to fight against me with a sword. But I'm coming against you in the name of the LORD who rules over all." David ran quickly to the battle line. He reached into his bag, took out a stone and slung it at Goliath. The stone hit him on the forehead and sank into it. He fell to the ground, dead.

> Don't let anyone lose hope because of that Philistine.

73

Wow!

God helped a little guy do really big things!

Larry learned how to ride a skateboard. And he learned how to play the harmonica, too. It may be awhile before he can do both—especially on a big hill. But now he trusts that God will help him do all sorts of things he didn't think he could do!

Did you know that God can help you do really big things, too? If you love and trust him with all your heart, great things can happen!

After all...
God made you special and he loves you very much!

Hi boys and girls!

Bob called me selfish! I was making out my Christmas list. When I got to number seventy-three—a new pink plastic wind-up lobster to keep my blue wind-up lobster company—Bob got all huffy! He said I already had enough toys, AND enough toys to keep my other toys company. I didn't get it.

So Bob insisted it was time for another story! This one was about a king and his favorite toys!

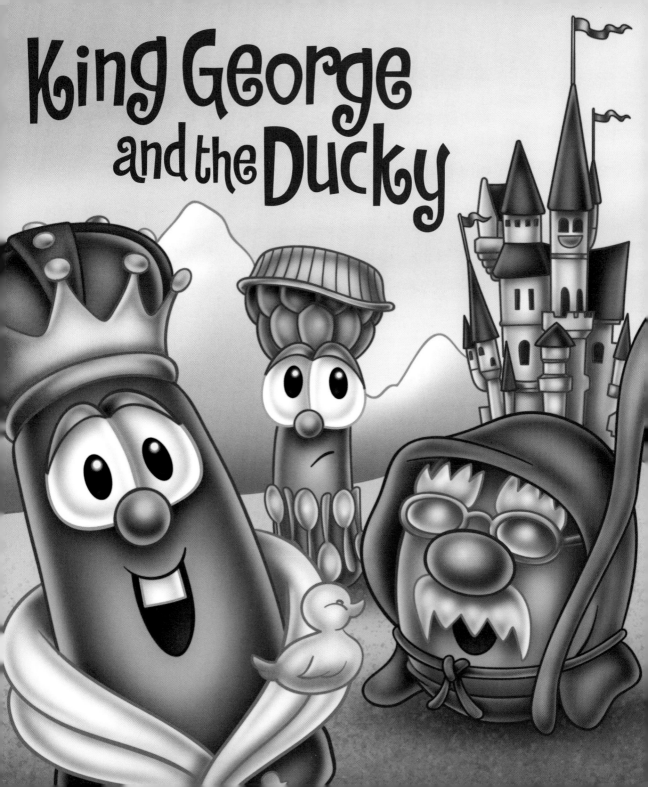

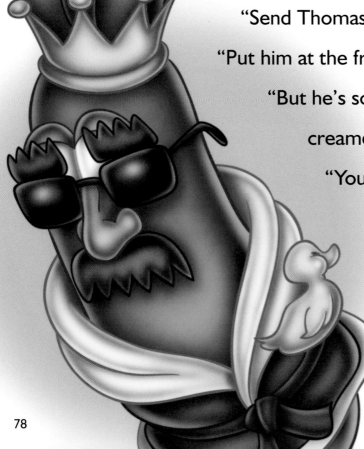

I must have it! I must get it!

King George loved rubber duckies. In fact, he had so many rubber duckies, he couldn't even count them all. But there was one ducky the king didn't have— Thomas' ducky.

"We need more men at the war front, sir!" said Cedric, the King's General.

"Send Thomas!" the king demanded. "Put him at the front of the battle!"

"But he's so small. He'll be creamed!" said Cedric.

"Your king has spoken!" said King George.

While Thomas was gone, the king snuck inside his house and took his ducky!

When King George got home, there was a knock at his door.

"Thomas was all alone on the front line, but he never gave up!" Cedric reported to the king. "He's a war hero. But I'm afraid he got creamed!"

King George didn't care. He just wanted to take a bath with his new ducky! Suddenly a wise man named Melvin came to the castle to tell the king a story.

The kingdom was at war— the great Pie War, to be exact.

Melvin began his story, "There once was a man, a very rich man. He had a lot of sheep. He had a lot of land. He threw a lot of parties. He was a very rich man.

"There was another man, a very poor man. He had next to nothing, just a little lamb. He loved it like a son, and he fed it from his hand.

"Yes, he was a very poor man.

"One day there was a guest at the house of the rich man. What did he do to feed the guest of the rich man?"

"He had plenty of sheep," said King George. "He could share his."

Melvin continued: "Wrong! He took the lamb of the poor man."

"Who is this rich man who did this terrible thing?" ordered King George.

"You are that man!" said Melvin.

You were only thinking about yourself and what you wanted!

Now I know just what to do! Before I think about me, I'd better think about you!

"You have many duckies. Thomas only had one. You were selfish and took it."

King George felt bad.

"God wants us to think of others first. When we're selfish, we hurt the people around us."

"What should I do?" asked King George.

"Ask God to forgive you," Melvin explained. "Ask Thomas to forgive you and make it right."

"Draw me a bath!" said King George to his servant.

"I've gotta find Thomas!"

Thomas had never had a more wonderful bath, especially when King George gave his rubber ducky back!

King George told Thomas he was sorry and asked Thomas to forgive him. Then he prayed and asked God to forgive him, too!

King George felt better after doing what was right. From then on he always tried not to be selfish, and to think of others first. End

The Bible Story

God doesn't want us to be selfish! He wants us to think about other people before we think about ourselves. A man named David learned that same lesson in the Bible.

David's Selfish Sin

selections from 2 Samuel 12:1-13

The LORD sent the prophet Nathan to David. Nathan said, "Two men lived in the same town. One was rich. The other was poor. The rich man had a very large number of sheep and cattle. But all the poor man had was one little female lamb. He had bought it. He raised it. It grew up with him and his children. It shared his food. It drank from his cup. It even slept in his arms.

One day a traveler came to the rich man. The rich man wanted to prepare a meal for him. But he didn't want to kill one of his own sheep or cattle. Instead, he took the little female lamb that belonged to the poor man. Then he cooked it for the traveler who had come to him."

David burned with anger against the rich man. He said to Nathan, "The man who did that is worthy of death. The man must pay back four times as much as that lamb was worth. How could he do such a thing? And he wasn't even sorry he had done it."

The LORD has taken away your sin.

Then Nathan said to David, "You are the man! The LORD, the God of Israel, says, 'I made you king over the people of Israel and Judah. Why did you turn your back on what I told you to do? You did what is evil in my sight. You made sure that Uriah, the Hittite, would be killed in battle. You took his wife to be your own. You let the men of Ammon kill him with their swords.' " Then David said to Nathan, "I have sinned against the LORD." Nathan replied, "The LORD has taken away your sin."

Amazing!

Bob was right! I told him I was sorry for being so greedy. From now on, I'm going to share everything—even my hairbrush (although Bob won't need it).

I'm also planning on turning my seventy-three-item Christmas list into a list of seventy-three things I can *give* to others, instead. I think that's what God would want, because he wants us to think of others—and give to others—not just think of all that we can get for ourselves!

After all ...
God made you special and he loves you very much!

Don't do anything only to get ahead ... Instead, be free of pride. Think of others as better than yourselves.

— Philippians 2:3

Hello boys and girls!

I've really got a dilemma. A very good friend of mine is always getting teased. Just because she's an onion, the other kids call her Smelly Kelly. It's so mean. I know that I should stick up for her, but I'm afraid that if I do the kids will tease me then, too. I really don't know what to do.

Bob tried to help me. He told me that I shouldn't be afraid to do what's right. Then he gave me a story to read: the story of Esther, the Girl Who Became Queen.

So do not be afraid. We need not run and hide.

A long time ago, the king of Persia decided to choose a new queen. Ladies came from all over the kingdom to appear before King Xerxes in a competition for the crown.

One girl, Esther of Babylon, sang so beautifully of God's love that the king chose her to be his new queen. But Queen Esther was not happy about her new position.

"Esther, you're the queen of all Persia!" her cousin Mordecai exclaimed. "You gotta be at least a little excited!'

"But I don't want to be queen!" Esther cried.

"Oh, Esther, God has a plan for you," he told her. "There must be a reason that you're the queen."

Mordecai, who worked as a palace guard, was very wise and faithful to God.

There is nothing we can't face when God is on our side.

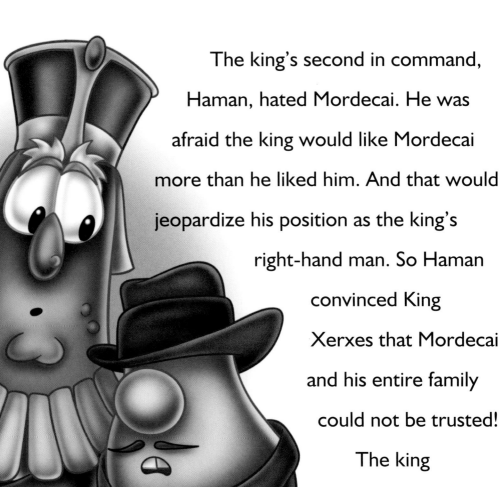

The king's second in command, Haman, hated Mordecai. He was afraid the king would like Mordecai more than he liked him. And that would jeopardize his position as the king's right-hand man. So Haman convinced King Xerxes that Mordecai and his entire family could not be trusted! The king banished Mordecai's entire family to the Island of Perpetual Tickling! (That's the island where you are tickled day and night, night and day, without stopping!)

The law must be adjusted.

Mordecai said, "Esther! You must tell the king that my people are your people, or we'll all be banished!"

"I can't! You know what happens to people who appear before the king uninvited!" said Esther.

"You never have to be afraid to do what's right, Essie. Only you can save us. Perhaps this is the reason you became queen," Mordecai explained. "Perhaps God put you here for such a time as this!"

There are those who can't be trusted!

The battle
is not ours.
We look to
God above.

Esther was very afraid to go before the king. But she knew what she had to do, so the next day she timidly approached the throne.

"C'mon over here, Queenie Pooh!" the king said with a smile. (The king really liked Esther.) "Whatever you want is yours."

So Esther gathered up her courage and said, "Haman has lied to you about Mordecai. Mordecai is a good person. And his family is my family."

King Xerxes was stunned. He loved his queen and would never harm her people.

So the king told the Grim Tickler to take Haman to the Island of Perpetual Tickling, and Mordecai became his new right-hand man!

And that is the story of Esther, the girl who became queen and saved her people —all because she had the courage and faith to do what was right! **End**

He will guide us safely through and guard us with his love.

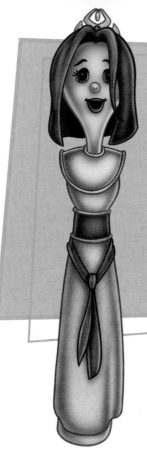

The Bible Story

You have to be very brave to do what's right. But it's important to trust in God's plan and remember that he will never leave your side. You can read about Esther's story in the Bible in the book named after her!

Esther's Story
selections from Esther 2-8

The king's attendants said, "King Xerxes, let a search be made for some beautiful young [women]. Then let the one who pleases you the most become queen." The king liked Esther more than he liked any of the other women. So he put a royal crown on her head [and] made her queen ...

Esther stood in the inner courtyard of the palace. The king was sitting on his royal throne. He reached out toward her the gold rod that was in his hand. Then Esther approached him [and] touched the tip of the rod. The king asked, "What is it, Queen Esther? What do you want? I'll give it to you." Esther replied, "King Xerxes, if it pleases you, come to a big dinner today. I've prepared it for you. Please have Haman come with you." So the king and Haman went to the big dinner Esther had prepared.

Then Queen Esther [said], "King Xerxes, please spare my people. That's my appeal to you. My people and I have been sold to be destroyed. We've been sold to be killed and wiped out." King Xerxes asked [her], "Who is the man who has dared to do such a thing? And where is he?" Esther said, "The man hates us! He's our enemy! He's this evil Haman!" The king got up. He was burning with anger. The king said to his men, "Put Haman to death!"

King Xerxes, please spare my people.

The Jews in every city could now gather together and fight for their lives. The king's order gave them that right. They celebrated.

Wow!

I'm really glad Bob helped me remember the importance of having courage. I needed to be reminded that God is always by my side and I should never be afraid as long as I'm doing what's right.

Next time I see the kids picking on Kelly, I'm going to stand by her side and help her. That's what God would want me to do! And besides, just because she's an onion doesn't mean she smells. I've known some pretty stinky cucumbers, too! But God loves them all!

Remember...
God made you
    special and he
loves you very much!

99

Hey boys and girls!

Larry gave me a daisy to celebrate May Day. Daisies are swell. But I noticed that Laura Carrot got a whole bouquet of tulips. Mr. Nezzer received a sizable fern in a hanging pot, and Pa Grape got a whole basket full of peonies. I don't mean to be ungrateful, but just one daisy?

Larry reminded me of a great story we did a long time ago. It's about a very unthankful blueberry.

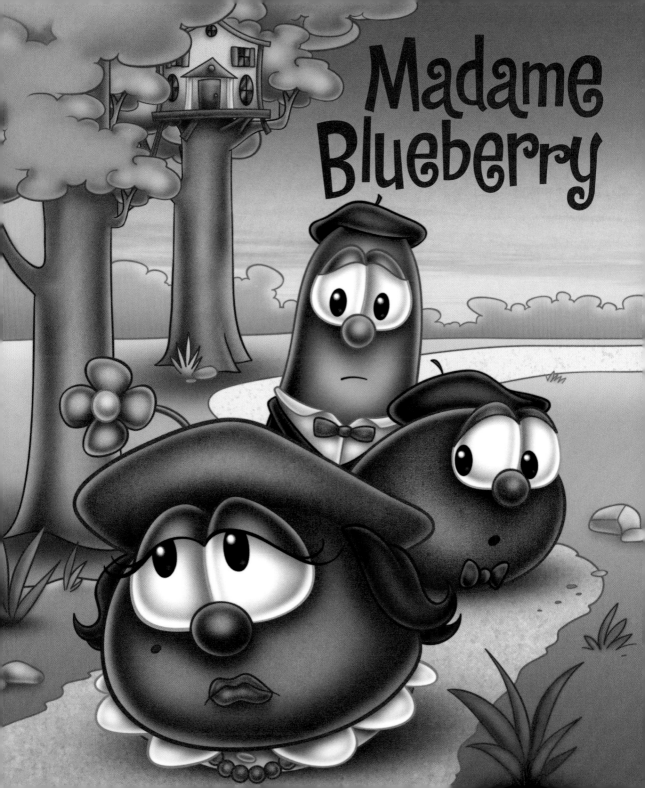

Every morning, Madame Blueberry gazed longingly at photos of her neighbor's stuff. "Look at this new flatware of Monsieur Lagoon's," she cried, "and Monsieur Desplanes has twelve Franklin Mint spoons ..." She was a very blue berry.

"I'm so blue-hoo-hoo, blue-hoo-hoo, blue-hoo-hoo!" she cried. "I'm so blue I don't know what to do!"

One day the doorbell rang. Butler Bob opened the door.

"Allow us to introduce ourselves," they sang. "We're neighbors. We moved in down the street. Some say we're the most delightful bunch of fellows you'll ever want to meet!"

All you need is lots more stuff!

"We represent the Stuff-Mart, a magic land of retail. Would you care to see what's on sale?"

"If I buy more things, will that make me happy?" asked Madame Blueberry.

"Yes, happiness awaits you at Stuff-Mart," the salesmen said.

So she dashed off to the store, with her butlers Bob and Larry right behind.

A thankful heart is a happy heart.

On their way to the store, they saw a little girl celebrating her birthday in the park with her family. All the little girl got for her birthday was a single piece of apple pie and a bowl of oatmeal. But she was so happy. She sang, "I thank God for this day, for the sun in the sky, for my mom and my dad, for my piece of apple pie!"

Madame Blueberry was confused. The little girl had so little and yet she was HAPPY? She would think about this later. Right now, it was time to shop.

Inside the front door of the Stuff-Mart, Madame Blueberry saw everything she had ever wanted! As she filled cart after cart, she saw a small boy with his father.

"Dad! Can I have this train set, please?" he asked.

"We can't afford that, Junior. How about a nice bouncy ball?"

Thank you, Dad, for our day, and my big, red, bouncy ball!

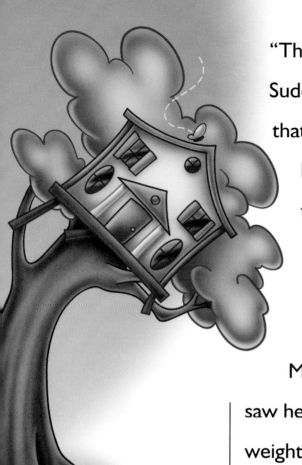

"Thanks, Dad!" the little boy smiled. Suddenly Madame Blueberry realized that she didn't want all the stuff she bought. Instead, she wanted what that little boy in the store had, and what that little girl in the park had. She wanted a happy heart!

As she began to leave the Stuff-Mart, she looked down the valley and saw her treehouse start to bend under the weight of all her new stuff!

Bob, Larry, and Madame Blueberry rushed towards the house. As they watched, a butterfly landed on top of the roof. The weight of the butterfly was too much.

The treehouse bent all the way to the

We say thanks every day!

ground and the stuff started to fall out! Then it snapped back up and her house went flying!

Madame Blueberry lost her whole house and all the stuff in it, but she wasn't blue. She realized how thankful she was for everything she did have—especially her friends! End

This once very blueberry was truly thankful that day.

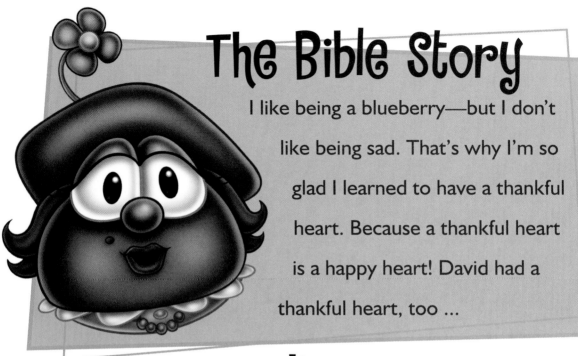

The Bible Story

I like being a blueberry—but I don't like being sad. That's why I'm so glad I learned to have a thankful heart. Because a thankful heart is a happy heart! David had a thankful heart, too ...

David's Heart
Psalm 34

Ps 34:1 I will thank the Lord at all times.

My lips will always praise him.

Ps 34:2 I will honor the Lord.

Let those who are hurting hear and be joyful.

Ps 34:3 Join me in giving glory to the Lord.

Let us honor him together.

Ps 34:4 I looked to the Lord, and he answered me.

He saved me from everything
I was afraid of.

Ps 34:5 Those who look to
him beam with joy.

Ps 34:6 This poor man called
out, and the LORD heard
him.

He saved him out of all of his
troubles.

Ps 34:8 Taste and see that the
LORD is good.

Blessed is the man who goes
to him for safety.

Ps 34:9 You people of God,
have respect for the LORD.

Those who respect him have
everything they need.

Ps 34:11 My children, come.
Listen to me.

I will teach you to have
respect for the LORD.

Ps 34:14 Turn away from evil,
and do good.

Look for peace, and go
after it.

Ps 34:17 Godly people cry
out, and the LORD hears
them.

He saves them from all of
their troubles.

Ps 34:19 Anyone who does
what is right may have
many troubles.

But the LORD saves him from
all of them.

Oh, yes!

I want to be thankful like the little girl who had pie on her birthday, the little boy who got a ball, and Madame Blueberry, who had good friends. She was thankful even when she lost her treehouse.

In fact, I want to tell Larry how thankful I am for getting this pretty daisy! I'm glad he's my friend.

What are you thankful for? Remember what you're thankful for every day. Then you'll have a happy heart, too! And here's something else for you to be thankful for:

God made you special and he loves you very much!

Give thanks to the Lord, because he is good. His faithful love continues forever.

— Psalm 118:1

Hi kids!

The other day at the park, a bunch of bullies were teasing Jean Claude about his French accent. They tried to get Bob and me to join in. They even said if we didn't, they'd take our lunches! Well, it was Tuesday so I had made my specialty—peanut butter and swiss cheese sandwiches. So we REALLY didn't want our lunches to get taken.

That's when Bob reminded me of a story about three guys who found themselves in a pickle of their own.

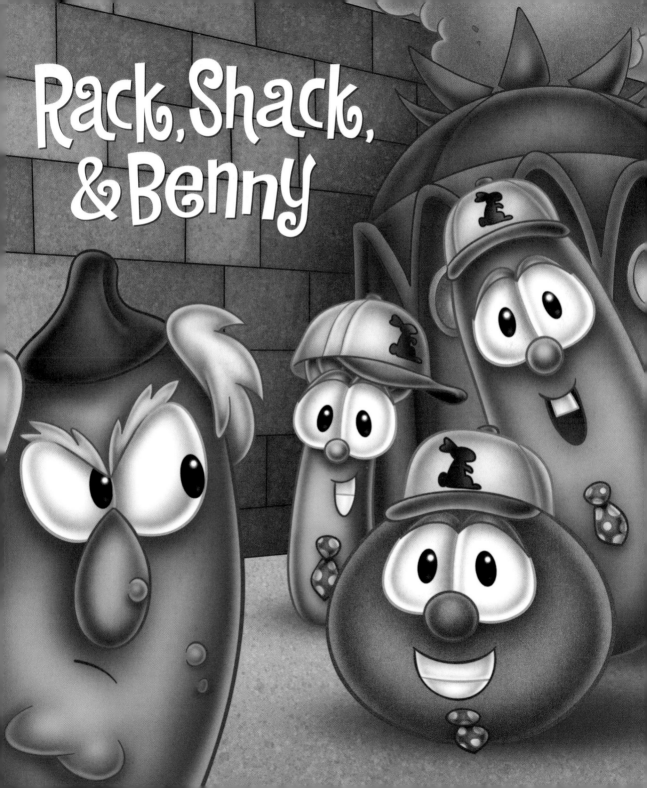

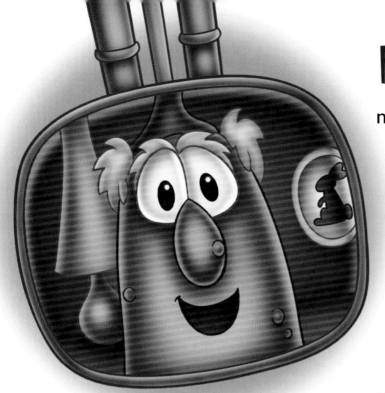

The bunny,
the bunny.
Whoa,
I love the
bunny!

For the next thirty minutes, you may eat as many chocolate bunnies as you want!" Mr. Nezzer announced to everyone at the Nezzer Chocolate Factory. He was celebrating the two millionth chocolate bunny to ship from the factory.

Everyone began eating!

"Wait!" said Shack. "Our parents taught us that too much candy isn't good for us!"

Rack, Shack, and Benny loved to eat chocolate bunnies. But they agreed that it wasn't right to eat too many.

Even if all the other workers kept eating and eating ...

Soon, the others all had stomach aches. When Mr. Nezzer saw that Rack, Shack, and Benny were still standing, he promoted them to junior executives!

Rack, Shack, and Benny were proud that they stood up for what was right!

Stand up! Stand up! For what you believe in!

All you gotta do is sing one little song.

The next day, Mr. Nezzer showed Rack, Shack, and Benny a surprise. He was building a 90-foot bunny!

"When my bunny is finished," he said with pride, "everyone will bow down before it and sing the Bunny Song!"

Rack, Shack, and Benny knew that God didn't want them to bow before anything but him. Yet, if they refused, Mr. Nezzer said he would throw them into the furnace!

When the bunny was finished, it was time for Rack, Shack, and Benny to bow down and sing the Bunny Song.

The Bible
tells us
what it's all
about!

"Sing it!" Mr. Nezzer ordered.

"We must stand up for what we believe, Mr. Nezzer," the junior executives said. "And we believe in God!"

"Throw them into the fiery furnace!" Mr. Nezzer shouted.

Do you
go along?
Even
though
the things
they
do are
wrong?

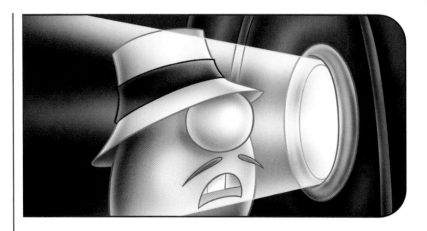

Rack, Shack, and Benny were tossed into the fiery furnace!

"Hey, boss," said Mr. Lunt, "they're not burning up!"

Mr. Nezzer looked inside the furnace and realized God was taking care of Rack, Shack, and Benny. "Come on out of there!" he shouted.

"What was I thinking?" asked Mr. Nezzer. "I'm sorry, boys. God saved you from the fiery furnace. Can you ever forgive me?"

"We forgive you, Mr. Nezzer," Rack, Shack, and Benny told him.

And that's the story of three boys who learned that if they stand up for what they believe in, God will stand with them! **End**

The Bible Story

When kids are trying to make you do stuff you don't want to do, it's not always easy to stand up for what you believe in! But it's important to remember that God wants you to do what's right. It will always be worth it in the end!

Shadrach, Meshach and Abednego
selections from Daniel 3:1-30

King Nebuchadnezzar made a statue that was covered with gold. A messenger called out, "You will soon hear ... all kinds of music. When you do, you must fall down and worship the gold statue. If you don't, you will be thrown into a blazing furnace."

As soon as the people heard the sound, they fell down and worshiped the gold statue. Shadrach, Meshach and Abednego [refused] to worship it. The king burned with anger. The men said, "We might be thrown into the blazing furnace. But the God we serve is able to bring us out of it alive. He will save us from your powerful hand. But … even if we knew that our God wouldn't save us, we still wouldn't serve your gods." The king's anger burned against [them]. He ordered that the furnace be heated seven times hotter than usual. He [commanded] some of the strongest soldiers in his army to tie up Shadrach, Meshach and Abednego. Then he told his men to throw them into the blazing furnace. Then the king leaped to his feet [and said,] "Look! I see four men walking around in the fire. They aren't tied up. And the fire hasn't even harmed them. The fourth man looks like a son of the gods." The king shouted, "You who serve the Most High God, come here!" The fire hadn't harmed their bodies. Their robes weren't burned either. And they didn't even smell like smoke. Then Nebuchadnezzar said, "May the God of Shadrach, Meshach and Abednego be praised!"

> The God we serve is able to bring us out … alive.

Meanwhile, at the park ...

So, Bob and I stood up for what we believe in! It was a little scary. That big old bully tried to take our lunches!

That's when I started singing Silly Songs. Pretty soon everybody was singing about hairbrushes, cebus, and water buffalos!

So kids, if you have to make a decision to stand up for what you believe in, always remember that God will be standing right there with you. It's another reminder of how ...

God made you special and he loves you very much!

Be on your guard.

Stand firm in the faith.

Be brave. Be strong.

—1 Corinthians 16:13

Hey kids!

Have you ever tried to make a really tough decision? Making tough decisions is something that I'm just not very good at. Like the time I had to decide between getting a baby kangaroo and a water buffalo. Who can make a decision like that?

Well, actually, I guess that's not really the kind of decision I'm talking about. I'm talking about the kind of decision when you know what you SHOULD do, but it would be easier to do something else. Bob said it would help if we read the story of Daniel.

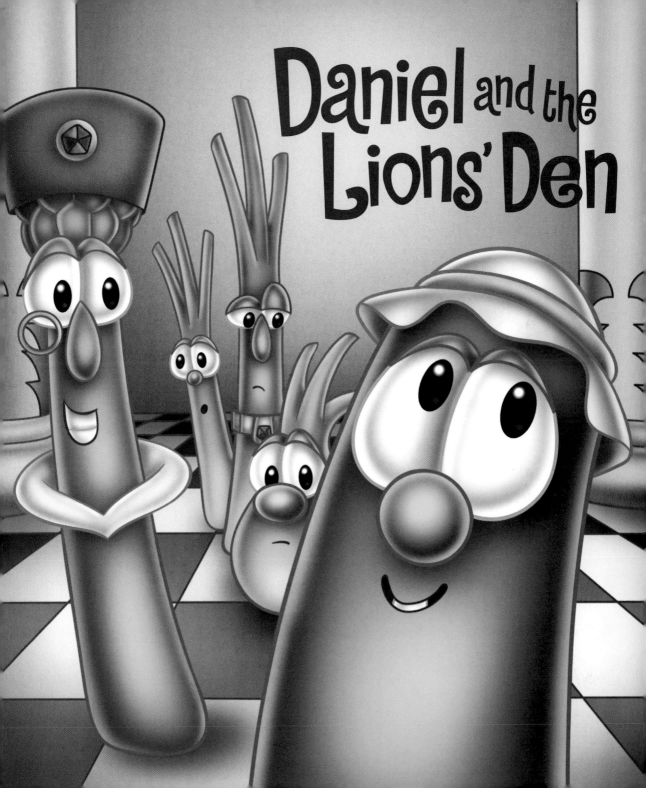

There is
one who is
wiser still,
and Daniel
is his name.
So before
you take
another
sleeping pill,
perhaps he
can explain.

Long ago in the city of Babylon, there lived a wise, young man named Daniel. Daniel worked hard in the palace of the Babylonian king. One night, while the kingdom slept, the king had a dream.

"I am King Darius," the king reported. "I've had a dream. And now I'm feeling rather frightened and I wish someone would tell me what it means."

"We are your wise men," the three sleepy scallions explained. "Yes, that is true. And though we're using all our wisdom, we're afraid we can't explain your dream to you."

So the king sent for Daniel. And with God's help, Daniel was able to explain the king's dream.

"Daniel, you have enlightened me. Your job I will expand. From now on, I want you to sit right beside me as the second in command."

Daniel's new job made the wise scallions very jealous. They didn't want to take orders from Daniel. So they came up with a sneaky plan to get rid of him.

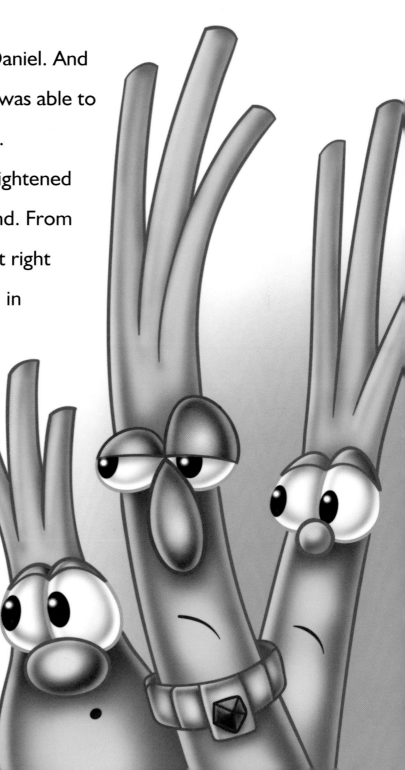

Oh, no!
What we
gonna do?

The next morning, the scallions convinced the king to pass a new law. They knew this law would catch Daniel.

"Just one more time, now let's see if I've got this straight," the asparagus king repeated. "A law to prove once and for all that I am great. If I'm the king, no one must doubt my full supremacy. So from this day forth, my citizens will pray to only ME."

So the law was passed and that's when Daniel's troubles started.

You see, God's law required that his people worship only God. And Daniel always obeyed God's law.

So the next day, just like always, Daniel prayed to God.

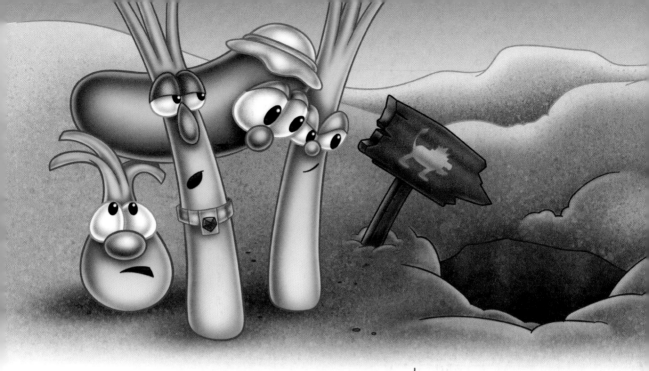

He was thanking him for giving him the courage to do what's right when ... WHAM! The three scallions broke into Daniel's room and carried him away.

"Daniel, you have violated section 42192R94 thousand, 6, dot, one, dash, 7B of the code of Babylon," the tallest scallion yelled. Then he threw Daniel into the den of lions.

Hey, Daniel! You're sure gonna have fun down there. We're not 'ly-in'!

Deep in the dark, scary lions' den, Daniel could hear the lions roar and he could see their eyes blinking in the dark. He was frightened. But then he heard a voice. It was an angel.

"Don't cry, Daniel. Fear not, Daniel. Don't you know you're not alone?"

The angel reminded Daniel that God was with him ... even there in the lions' den. This made Daniel feel much better.

The next morning, the king and his trusted wise men ran to the den.

"Hellooooo!!!" the king shouted.

Though it seems this time you won't get through, God has made a way!

"I'll be right up! I just have to say goodbye to my new friends," Daniel shouted back.

To everyone's surprise, Daniel had not been harmed!

"Surely your God is above all men. Now I understand," King Darius proclaimed. "For even at the bottom of the lions' den, you were in his hand."

The king passed a new law declaring that everyone should pray only to Daniel's God.

The wise men were in big trouble, so they moved to Egypt!

But Daniel stayed, and God blessed him all his days. End

Surely your God is above all men!

The Bible Story

God is always with us. He watches over us and he loves us. And he wants us to do what's right.

Take one more look at Daniel's story.

Daniel's Story

selections from Daniel 6:1-28

Daniel did a better job than any of the royal rulers. So the king planned to put him in charge of the whole kingdom. But the [others] heard about it [and] looked for a reason to bring charges against Daniel. They went as a group to the king [and suggested that he should give this] order: "During the next 30 days don't let any of your people pray to any god or man except to you. If they do, throw them into the lions' den."

Daniel did just as he had always done before. He went to his room three times a day to pray. He got down on his knees and gave thanks to his God. When the king heard that, he didn't want Daniel to be harmed in any way. Then the men went as a group to the king [and said,] "Remember that no order or law you make can be changed." So the king [had] Daniel brought out and thrown into the lions' den. The king said to him, "You always serve your God faithfully. So may he save you!"

Has he saved you from the lions?

As soon as the sun began to rise, the king hurried to the lions' den. He called out to Daniel. "You serve the living God. Has he [saved] you from the lions?" Daniel answered, "My God sent his angel [to] shut the mouths of the lions. They haven't hurt me at all! The king ordered his servants to lift Daniel out of the den. Then King Darius wrote to the people from every nation and language in the whole world. He said, "I order people in every part of my kingdom to respect and honor Daniel's God."

Decisions, decisions...

That was a great story! Daniel was very brave because he knew that if he did what was right, God would protect him. Even in the depths of the lions' den!

Sure makes me feel better. I don't think I've ever been in THAT much trouble before. I mean, maybe I've been in a den with a bunch of water buffaloes. But they're pretty easy to get along with, really. Especially if you have chocolate in your pocket!

Remember...
God made you special and he loves you very much!

Stand firm. Hold on to
what we taught you.
— 2 Thessalonians 2:15

Hello there!

I always try my hardest, no matter what I'm doing. But sometimes no matter how hard I try, I seem to mess things up ... just a little bit. The other day I was painting the sets for our next show when the skateboard I was standing on flew out from under me. I spilled a whole bucket of blue paint right on Bob's head.

He was really mad. I told him I could fix it, but he just told me there would be no second chances for me. I told him it was time to read the story of Jonah!

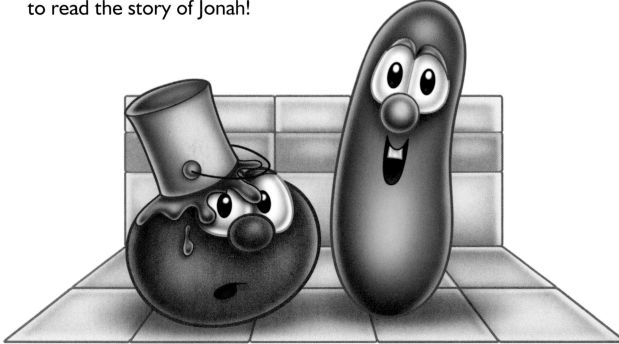

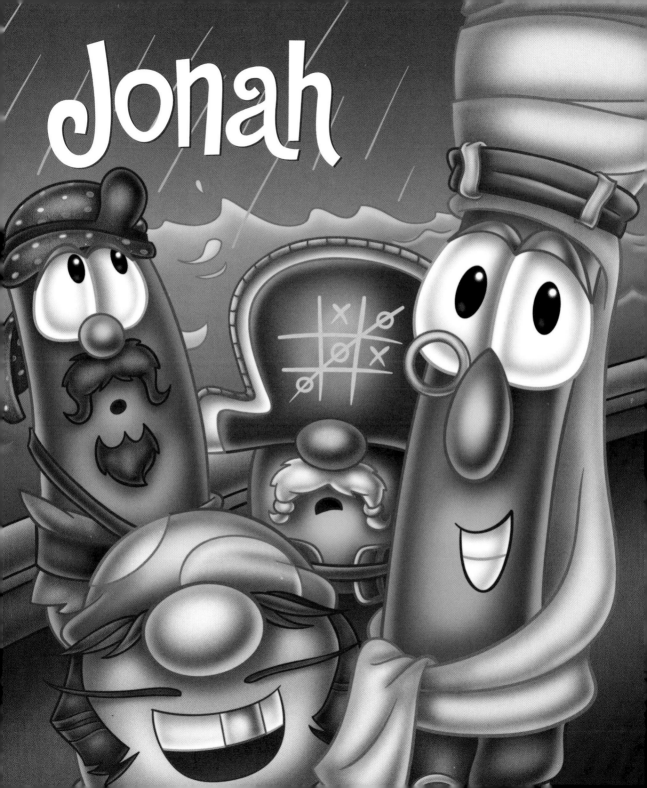

Jonah was a prophet of God. That meant that he was one of the very special people that God used to deliver messages. One night Jonah got a message from God that was supposed to be delivered to the biggest, meanest city around—Nineveh. The people of Nineveh were known for lying, cheating, and slapping each other with fish. They were so mean that Jonah and all the people of Israel wished that God would just wipe Nineveh off the face of the earth! Jonah didn't want to go to Nineveh.

The next day, Jonah hopped onboard a ship headed in the opposite direction. The ship belonged to those lazy scallywags, The Pirates Who Don't Do Anything. As the four new friends were sailing along, the sky got dark and the wind began to blow. CRASH went the thunder! FLASH went the lightning! SPLASH went the waves.

"This is a storm like I've never seen before!" yelled Captain Grape. "Somebody up there must be really upset with somebody down here!"

If we don't do something quick, we're gonna sink!

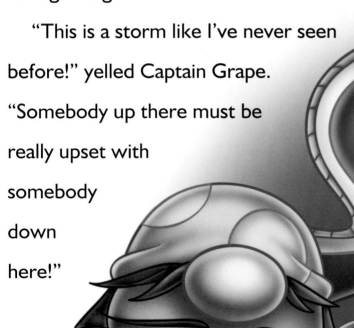

Oh Lord, don't let us die for this man's sin.

That somebody was Jonah because he had ignored God's directions. To get the storm to stop, the pirates made Jonah walk the plank.

SPLASH! Into the water he went.

As soon as Jonah hit the water, the storm cleared and the sun came back out.

The Pirates tried to pull Jonah back onto the boat but before they could ...

GULP! Jonah was swallowed up by a HUGE fish!

Jonah sat alone inside the whale. He was sure that he was going to die.

Suddenly, a bunch of angels appeared. "Jonah," the angels said, "we've got a message for you."

"If you say you're sorry for all the stuff you do," the angels sang, "you know God will be ready with a second chance for you!"

The angels reminded Jonah of God's great mercy. So from inside the whale, Jonah prayed and he told God he was sorry and asked him for a second chance.

God is the God of second chances!

BURP! Three days later that big fish spit Jonah out. Jonah had been given a second chance! So he headed straight to Nineveh to tell them about God's love. When he reached the gates of the city, the guards refused to let him in. "You're a stranger," they said. "We don't like strangers."

Jonah started to turn around and go home when he heard a familiar voice. "Jonah, is that you?" It was pirate Larry and his two lazy pirate friends!

A message for the whole city?

So The Pirates Who Don't Do Anything let Jonah into the city of Nineveh to deliver his message.

"Stop it!" he said to the king of Nineveh. "Stop cheating, stop lying, and especially stop slapping each other with fishes—or this entire city will be destroyed! A message from the Lord."

The king was very upset. No one told him they weren't supposed to do that stuff. The king made a decree for his people to stop what they were doing. God showed the people of Nineveh compassion and mercy. He gave them all a second chance! End

They stopped slapping each other with fishes!

The Bible Story

And so boys and girls, I hope that you see how important it is to give everyone a second chance. The fish slappers were sure happy they got a second chance! You can read the real story of Jonah in the Bible.

Jonah Runs Away
selections from Jonah 1-4

The LORD said, "Go to the city of Nineveh. Preach against it." But Jonah ran away. He found a ship and sailed [away]. The LORD sent a strong wind over the sea. A wild storm came up. The ship was in danger of breaking apart. The sailors were afraid [and] said, "Let's cast lots to find out who is to blame for getting us into all of this trouble." Jonah was picked. "Pick me up and throw me into the sea," [Jonah said]. "Then it will become calm."

They took Jonah and threw him overboard. And the stormy sea became calm.

The LORD sent a huge fish to swallow Jonah. And Jonah was inside the fish for three days and three nights. Jonah prayed to the LORD his God. The LORD gave the fish a command. And it spit Jonah up onto dry land. A message came to Jonah from the LORD a second time. He said, "Go to the great city of Nineveh. Announce to its people the message I give you." Jonah obeyed the LORD. The people of Nineveh believed God's warning [and] stopped doing what was evil. So [God] took pity on them. He didn't destroy them as he had said he would.

You are slow to get angry.

But Jonah was very upset [and] became angry. He prayed, "LORD, that's why I was so quick to run away. I knew that you are tender and kind. You are slow to get angry. You [take] pity on people." The LORD replied, "Do you have any right to be angry? Nineveh has more than 120,000 people. They can't tell right from wrong. So shouldn't I show concern for that great city?"

So, about that paint thing...

I have some good news and some really good news. First, Bob has showed me compassion and mercy! He realizes that I didn't spill the paint on purpose and he said he would give me a second chance. And, really, blue looks pretty good on a red tomato anyway. Don't you think?

But wait, there's more! The best news of all is that God is a God of second chances! All you have to do to get a second chance from God is ask.

Because...
God made you special and he loves you very much!

Be kind and tender to one another. Forgive each other, just as God forgave you because of what Christ has done.

— Ephesians 4:32

Hi everybody!

Every year around Christmas, Bob and I and all our friends get together and put on a Christmas pageant at our church. Have you ever done that? Glueing glitter all over everything always helps to get me in the Christmas spirit!

Well, this year I decided to write a poem about the production—you know, document my experience. So here it is, "The Stable that Bob Built!"

The Stable that Bob Built

Bob designed all the sets for the show!

This is the stable that Bob built.

This is the cow that mooed in the stable that Bob built.

These are the lambs, all cuddly and spry, that wandered off and followed the guy, who didn't know how to milk the cow that mooed in the stable that Bob built.

This is the shepherd,
who ate apple pie,
who cared for
the lambs, all
cuddly and spry,
that wandered off and
followed the guy, who didn't know how to
milk the cow that mooed in the stable that
Bob built.

Starring
Jimmy and
Jerry Gourd
as the cow!

It wasn't easy getting the cotton to stick onto the peas to make them look like sheep.

This is the angel who showed the way with a star to the three wise men who traveled so far. (It would have been easier if they'd had a car.)

She showed the way to the shepherd with pie, who cared for his lambs, all cuddly and spry, that wandered off and followed the guy, who didn't know how to milk the cow that mooed in the stable that Bob built.

This is the man, whom God designed, to love the woman so young and kind, that the angel told the shepherd to find.

She showed the way to the shepherd with pie, who cared for the lambs, all cuddly and spry, that wandered off and followed the guy, who didn't know how to milk the cow that mooed in the stable that Bob built.

Madame Blueberry made all the costumes. Aren't they great?

This is the baby, the Savior born, on that very first Christmas morn, the reason the star had shown the way for three wise men, who walked all day, to find the man, who God designed, to love the woman so young and kind, that the angel told the shepherd to find.

She showed the way to the shepherd with pie, who cared for the lambs, all cuddly and spry, that wandered off and followed the guy, who didn't know how to milk the cow that mooed in the stable that Bob built.

Larry played the part of a wise man... A very big stretch!

These are the Veggies who played the parts in the story that lives in all of our hearts, to share the news of the Savior born on that very first Christmas morn —all in the stable that Bob built! **End**

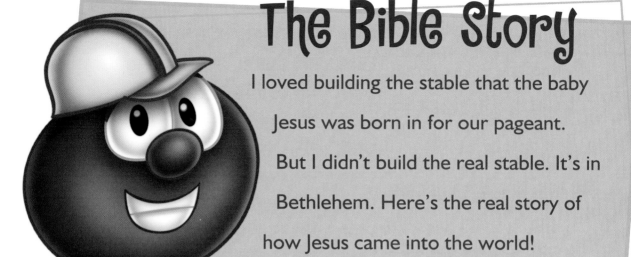

The Bible Story

I loved building the stable that the baby Jesus was born in for our pageant. But I didn't build the real stable. It's in Bethlehem. Here's the real story of how Jesus came into the world!

Jesus Is Born
selections from Luke 2:1-20

In those days, Caesar Augustus made a law. It required that a list be made of everyone in the whole Roman world. So Joseph went to Bethlehem, the town of David, because he belonged to the family line of David. He went there with Mary to be listed. Mary was engaged to him. She was expecting a baby. While [they] were there, the time came for the child to be born. She gave birth to her first baby. It was a boy. She wrapped him in large strips of cloth [and] placed him in a manger. There was no room for them in the inn.

There were shepherds living out in the fields nearby. An angel of the Lord appeared to them. And the glory of the Lord shone around them. They were terrified. But the angel said to them, "Do not be afraid. I bring you good news of great joy. It is for all the people. Today, in the town of David, a savior has been born to you. He is Christ the Lord. Here is how you will know I am telling you the truth. You will find a baby wrapped in strips of cloth and lying in a manger." Suddenly a large group of angels from heaven also appeared. They were praising God. They said, "May glory be given to God in the highest heaven! And may peace be given to those he is pleased with on earth!" Then the shepherds said to one another, "Let's go to Bethlehem. Let's see this thing that has happened, which the Lord has told us about." So they hurried off and found Mary and Joseph and the baby. The baby was lying in the manger.

He is Christ the Lord.

Well, that's my poem.

I sure hope you enjoyed my inside look at the VeggieTales Christmas pageant. We had a great time with the pageant this year! And Bob did such a great job on the sets. I mean, that stable is nicer than my house! I think I might just move into it until we need it for next year. We love sharing the message of Jesus' birth with everyone at our church. It's always such a great reminder of how...

God made you special and he loves you very much!

Hey boys and girls!

I don't know about you, but sometimes I'm scared of more things than I care to think about! That's why I turn on my LarryBoy flashlight when I go to bed.

Last night, my flashlight went OUT! If I had knees, they'd have been knocking! That's when Bob reminded me of the very first story we ever told; it's the story called Where's God When I'm S-Scared?

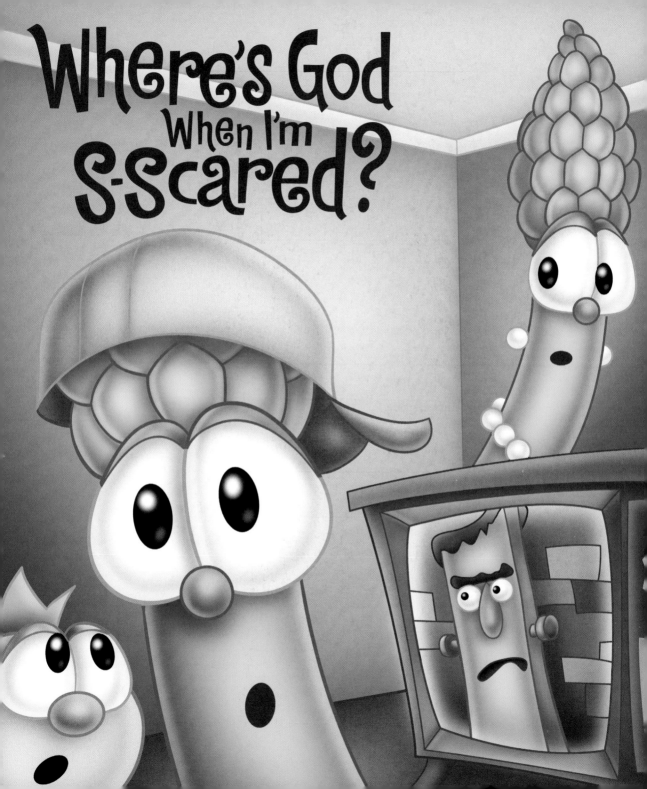

Were those eyeballs in the closet?

"Junior! It's time for bed," Mom Asparagus said. "Besides, that *Tales from the Crisper* TV show is too scary for you."

"I'm not s-scared," Junior answered as he turned off the television and climbed the stairs.

Junior was sitting in the darkness of his bedroom when suddenly CRASH! A big, red monster appeared out of nowhere!

WHAM!

Junior's toy chest flew open and out popped ... a baby pickle?

Junior was happy to realize it was Bob the Tomato and Larry the Cucumber. "We heard you were scared, so we thought we'd help!"

Bob and Larry sang a song about how God is bigger than any monster!

"You don't have to be afraid, because God is the BIGGEST!" Bob explained.

There was something big and hairy casting shadows on the wall!

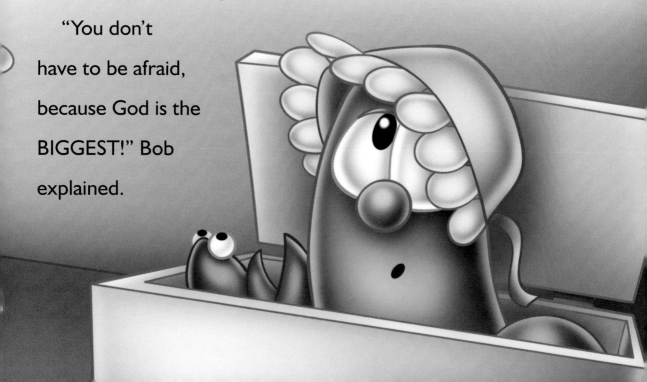

"Bigger than King Kong?" asked Junior. "Because King Kong's a really big monkey!"

"Next to God, King Kong would look like an itty bitty bug!" Bob said.

"Is he bigger than the Slime Monster?" Junior wondered. "Because he's the biggest monster of them all!"

"Compared to God, the Slime Monster is like a teeny, little corn flake," Larry said. "Just look in the sky!"

"God made all those stars out of nothing," Larry explained as they looked out the window.

"Wow!" Junior said. "The Slime Monster can't do that!"

"And God made the animals and all the

God is bigger than the boogie man! He's bigger than Godzilla!

people, too!" Bob continued. "That's why we don't have to be afraid. Everything God made is very special to him."

"So God's the biggest of all, and he's on my team!" Junior shouted.

... and he's watching out for you and me!

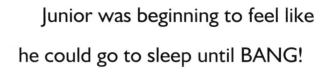

Junior was beginning to feel like he could go to sleep until BANG!

"Yikes! It's Frankencelery!" Junior screamed. The monster that scared Junior on the TV show jumped right into his bedroom.

"My name is Phil Winkelstein and I'm an actor from Toledo. I just pretend to be Frankencelery on television."

Junior couldn't believe it. All the monsters that Junior was afraid of weren't monsters at all. "Hey! What's all the racket?" Junior's dad asked, peeking in.

"Oh, I was just singing," Junior said. "God is bigger than any monster! He made the whole universe and he's taking good care of me, too!"

"That's right," his dad agreed. "It sounds like you're doing some good thinking. Now get some sleep. I love you, little mister."

"I love YOU, big mister!" said Junior.

And then, in the dark, Junior fell fast asleep. **End**

I know whatever's gonna happen, that God can handle it!

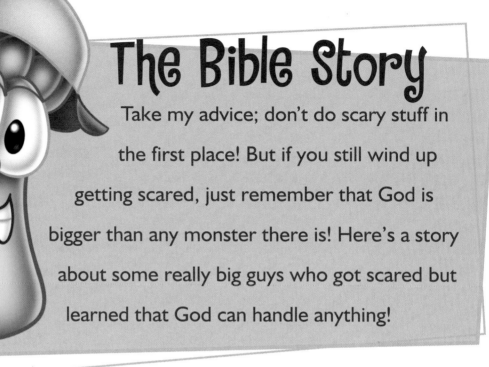

The Bible Story

Take my advice; don't do scary stuff in the first place! But if you still wind up getting scared, just remember that God is bigger than any monster there is! Here's a story about some really big guys who got scared but learned that God can handle anything!

Jesus Walks on Water
selections from Matthew 14:22-33

Right away Jesus made the disciples get into the boat. He had them go on ahead of him to the other side of the Sea of Galilee. Then he sent the crowd away. After he had sent them away, he went up on a mountainside by himself to pray. When evening came, he was there alone. The boat was already a long way from land. It was being pounded by the waves because the wind was blowing against it. Early in the morning, Jesus went out to the disciples. He walked on the lake. They saw him walking on the lake and were terrified. "It's a ghost!" they said. And they cried out in fear. Right away Jesus called out to them, "Be brave! It is I. Don't be afraid." "Lord, is it you?" Peter asked. "If it is, tell me to come to you on the water." "Come," Jesus said. So Peter got out of the boat. He walked on the water toward Jesus. But when Peter saw the

> **Right away Jesus called out to them, "Be brave! It is I. Don't be afraid."**

wind, he was afraid. He began to sink. He cried out, "Lord! Save me!" Right away Jesus reached out his hand and caught him. "Your faith is so small!" he said. "Why did you doubt me?" When they climbed into the boat, the wind died down. Then those in the boat worshiped Jesus. They said, "You really are the Son of God!"

It's true.

We all get scared sometimes. But it's really important to remember just how much God loves us! After all, God made absolutely everything! And God is going to take care of all those things and all those people he created.

As for me, I don't even need my LarryBoy flashlight anymore.

I hope you'll remember how much you're loved the next time you're scared!

After all ...
God made you special and he loves you very much!

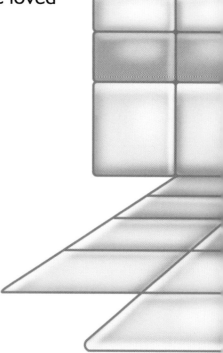

So do not be afraid.

I am with you.

— Isaiah 41:10

Hi there!

Today I saw two bikes crash. SMACK! Right into each other! It was a disaster. But what could I do?

First of all, I'm a busy guy. I have dance lessons and hairbrushes to find. There's my yodeling, my cebus, and my duckies! And don't forget that I'm a Pirate Who Doesn't Do Anything! So how can I possibly help them?

Junior had the answer. He remembered a very special story.

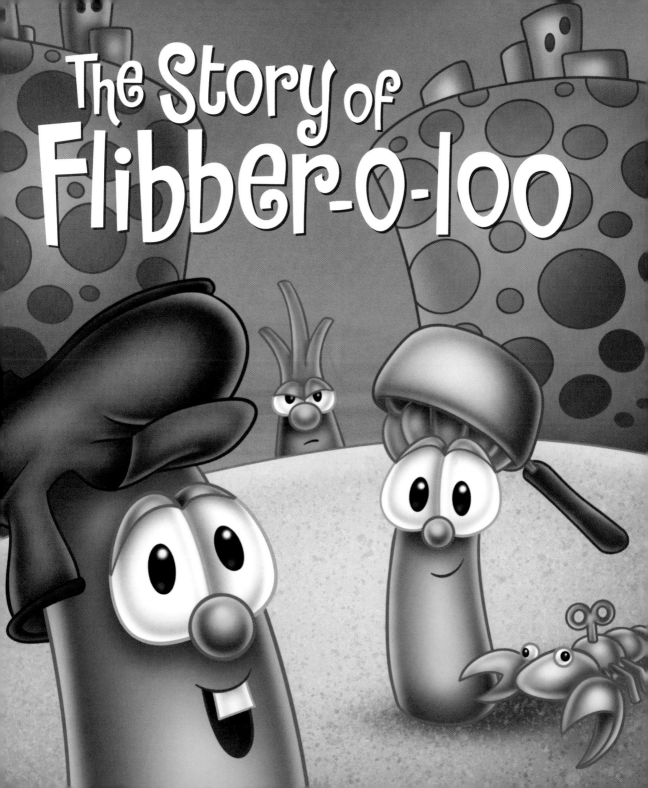

In a town to the west, called Flibber-o-loo, they thought they were best, cuz they wore a big shoe!

But those to the east in Jibber-de-lot disagreed with those folks, and instead, wore a pot! Till a shoe-headed boy and his blue plastic friend, went for a walk, down a slope, 'round a bend! And three shifty crooks jumped out from a rock—they knocked off his shoe, then they knocked off his sock!

But the thing they did next
was extremely un-funny: why
they shook him so hard that
he dropped his milk money!

But they didn't care—
they'd accomplished their
goal. So they put our friend
down—stuck his head in a
hole!

Things looked pretty
grim for our Flibbian
buddy, his head in a
hole, his shoe bent
and muddy.

But then were these footsteps? Oh,
could it be true? Along came the mayor of
Flibber-o-loo!

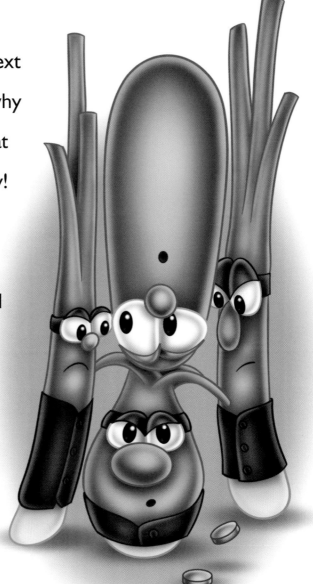

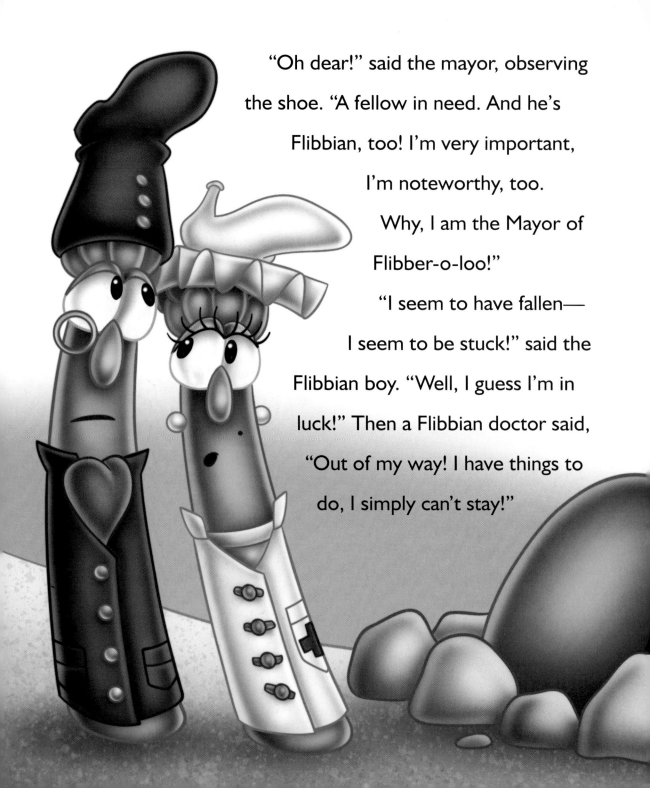

"Oh dear!" said the mayor, observing the shoe. "A fellow in need. And he's Flibbian, too! I'm very important, I'm noteworthy, too. Why, I am the Mayor of Flibber-o-loo!"

"I seem to have fallen— I seem to be stuck!" said the Flibbian boy. "Well, I guess I'm in luck!" Then a Flibbian doctor said, "Out of my way! I have things to do, I simply can't stay!"

Oh! It was dreadful. How could they desert their Flibbian friend with his head in the dirt?

"That's it, then ... I'm finished. I'll die here, down under. If they would not help me, then who would?" he wondered.

Then the boy with the pot saw our friend with the shoe. "Oh, look!" he exclaimed. "He's from Flibber-o-loo!"

He looked at our friend, and he looked at the shoe. And then in his heart, he knew what to do.

We're busy! Busy! Shockingly busy!

God
made us
special
and now
I can
see—If
you're
special to
him, then
you're
special to
me!

"He may be Flibbian, that's plain to see, but God made him special. Just like he made me!"

So he got him unstuck, and he picked up his shoe. And together, they walked back to Flibber-o-loo. They went to a doctor quite shocked by his pot. The Flibbian's friend was from Jibber-de-lot!

The boy with the pot paid the cucumber's bill. The Flibbians? They were touched by his goodwill! "If this little guy can take care of his brother, why can't we all try to help one another?"

So today if you visit the mountains of Flibble, you won't see a shoe or a pot. Instead they throw flowers and candy to nibble. I bet that you'd like it a lot! **End**

When you love your neighbor, loving means lending a hand!

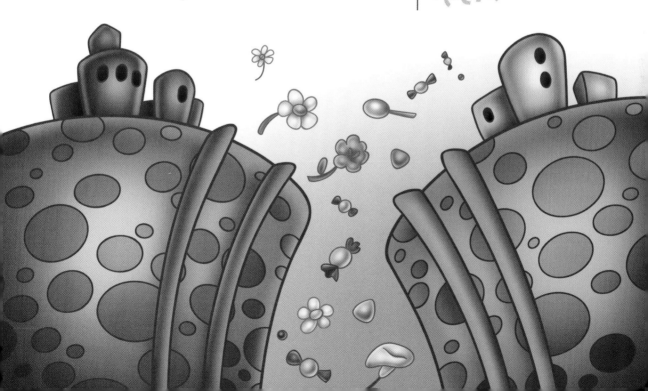

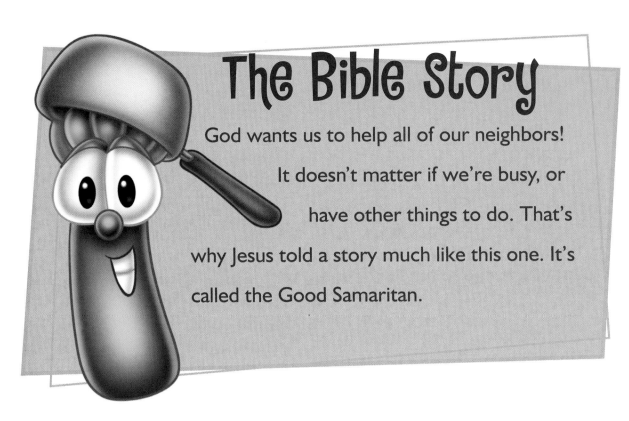

The Bible Story

God wants us to help all of our neighbors! It doesn't matter if we're busy, or have other things to do. That's why Jesus told a story much like this one. It's called the Good Samaritan.

The Good Samaritan
selections from Luke 10:30-37

Jesus [said], "A man was going down from Jerusalem to Jericho. Robbers attacked him. They stripped off his clothes and beat him. Then they went away, leaving him almost dead.

A priest happened to be going down that same road. When he saw the man, he passed by on the other side. A Levite also came by. When he saw the man, he passed by on the other side too. But a Samaritan came to the place where the man was. When he saw the man, he felt sorry for him. He went to him, poured olive oil and wine on his wounds and bandaged them. Then he put the man on his own donkey. He took him to an inn and took care of him. The next day he took out two silver coins. He gave them to the owner of the inn. 'Take care of him,' he said. 'When I return, I will pay you back for any extra expense you may have.'

> When he saw the man, he felt sorry for him ... He took him to an inn and took care of him.

Which of the three do you think was a neighbor to the man who was attacked by robbers?" The authority on the law replied, "The one who felt sorry for him." Jesus told him, "Go and do as he did."

Thanks, Junior!

We all need to be reminded that God wants us to love our neighbors. We all have other stuff we want to do. But loving each other is the most important thing!

So Junior and I scrounged around and found some bike tires, a couple of wrenches, and even an unopened box of chocolate cookies! We're heading over to help those guys who had that big bike crash. We can love others by following God's lead because ...

God made you special and he loves you very much!

I give you a new command. Love one another. You must love one another, just as I have loved you.

— John 13:34

183

Hi everybody!

Just because I get a little grumpy listening to "What We Have Learned" after every show, Larry told me that I don't appreciate music!

He really hurt my feelings. Sure, he *said* he was sorry. And I'm just supposed to forgive and forget. Well, no way, bucko!

Now Larry wants me to hear a story. Well, being the reasonable tomato that I am, I'll oblige.

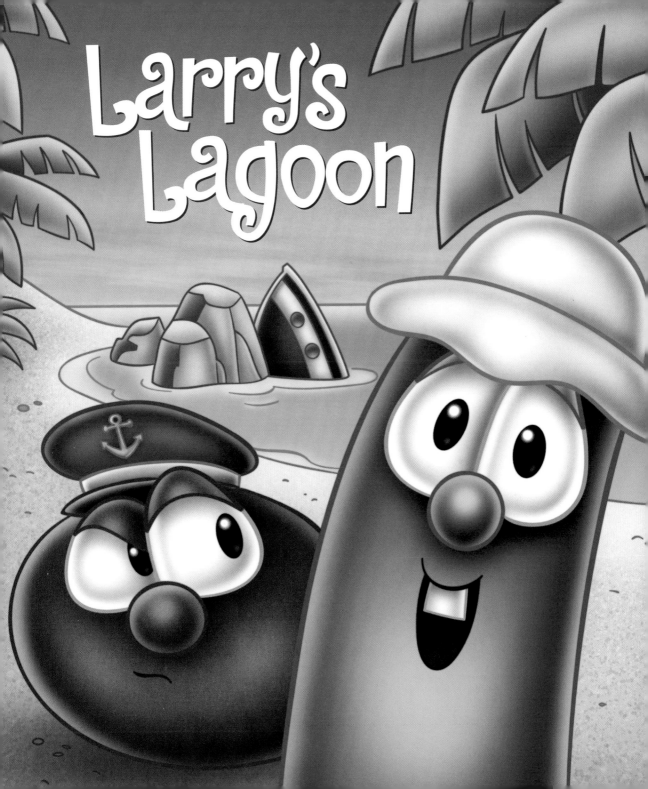

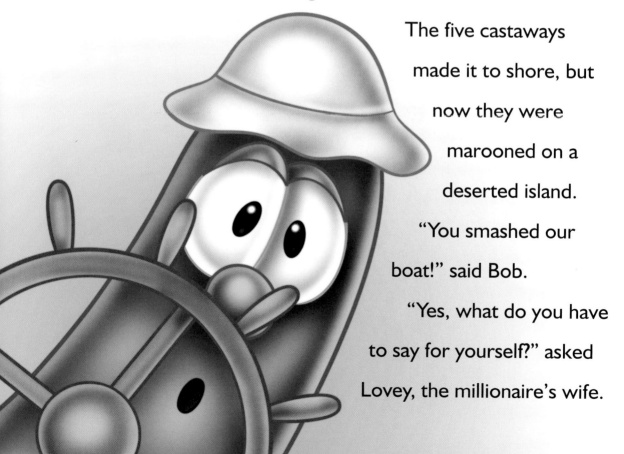

The
brochure
didn't say
anything
about this!

One summer Bob and Larry set sail on a three-hour tour with a millionaire, his wife, and a professor. Bob was the skipper and Larry was the first mate. But when Bob left the helm to check on their passengers, Larry crashed the boat right into a big rock!

The five castaways made it to shore, but now they were marooned on a deserted island. "You smashed our boat!" said Bob.

"Yes, what do you have to say for yourself?" asked Lovey, the millionaire's wife.

That night as they laid in their newly-constructed huts, Larry took a deep breath of the night air and said, "Gee, Bob, maybe this isn't so bad after all."

"Not bad? Larry, we're stuck on this island and we have no way to get home!"

"I said I was sorry," said Larry.

"Well, that's just not good enough!"

Larry was very sad. "He means I'M not good enough! I bet they'd be happier if I just left."

We most certainly had an accident. Someone has some explaining to do!

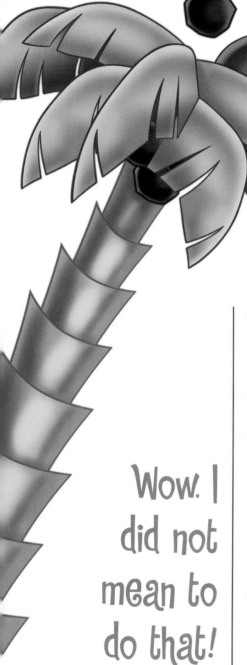

Wow. I did not mean to do that!

The next morning, the millionaire and Lovey saw the skipper up in a tree. "Has anyone seen Larry?" Bob asked. "When I woke up, he was gone!"

Suddenly the professor burst into the clearing with a giant bamboo catapult.

"If we wind it up and pull this cord, it will fling us back home!" he said, showing the castaways what he had made.

SPLOING!! A coconut shot into the air, knocked Bob out of the tree, and they both crashed through the roof of the millionaire's hut!

"I'm sorry!" said the professor. "Can you ever forgive me?"

"It was an accident," the skipper said. "I forgive you."

Then the skipper apologized to Lovey and the millionaire, too.

"We know you didn't mean to do it," said Lovey.

"We'll forgive you."

In love we
can forgive.
It is the
only way
to live!

"Boy, if I said I was sorry for doing something wrong and people still wouldn't forgive me, I'd feel terrible," he said.

Then they realized they hadn't forgiven Larry when he said he was sorry.

They ran down to the lagoon and found Larry floating away on a tiny raft.

"You guys don't like me anymore! So I'm just going to leave."

"But we DO like you!" said the millionaire. "And we forgive you for smashing the boat!" added Lovey.

"Everybody makes mistakes," the skipper said. "We were wrong not to forgive you when you said you were sorry."

"Oh! I forgive you guys!" said Larry.

WUBBA-WUBBA —it was the professor in a bamboo helicopter!

"Climb aboard!" said the professor.

Everyone was glad to be going home! They were also happy they had learned a great lesson about forgiveness, too.

Obey God and see that we can live in harmony!

The Bible Story

God sent Jesus to forgive us for our sins. And if God can forgive us, we should be able to forgive each other! Check out the story that Jesus told...

The Prodigal Son
selections from Luke 15:11-24

Jesus [said,] "There was a man who had two sons. The younger son [said,] 'Father, give me my share of the family property.' So the father divided his property [and money] between his two sons. The younger son packed up all he had [and] left for a country far away. There he wasted his money on wild living. He spent everything he had. Then the whole country ran low on food. So the son didn't have what he needed. He went to work for someone who sent him to the fields to feed the pigs. The son wanted to fill his stomach with the food the pigs were eating. But no one gave him anything. Then he began to think clearly again. He said, "Here I am dying from hunger! I will get up and go back to my father. I will say, 'Father, I have sinned against heaven. And I have sinned against you. I am no longer fit to be called your son. Make me like one of your hired workers.'"

He was lost. And now he is found.

"While the son was still a long way off, his father saw him. He was filled with tender love for his son. He ran to him. He threw his arms around him and kissed him. The son said to him, 'Father, I have sinned against heaven and against you. I am no longer fit to be called your son.' But the father said to his servants, 'Quick! Bring the best robe and put it on him. Put a ring on his finger and sandals on his feet. Let's have a big dinner and celebrate. This son of mine was dead. And now he is alive again. He was lost. And now he is found.'"

Larry! Where are you?

C'mon out! I forgive you! I really, really do!

You told me you were sorry and I should have forgiven you. You're my best buddy! I do all sorts of things wrong, too. I'm sure happy when I'm forgiven! And now, I hope you'll forgive me for not forgiving you.

I sure am glad that God forgives all of us!

After all ...
God made you special and he loves you very much!

Hey there!

I was shopping the other day, getting ready for Easter! I bought the biggest Easter basket I could find. And I got 182 multi-colored plastic eggs to fill with jellybeans and marshmallow chickens. And I got eight bags of green grass and four bags of purple!

I was very excited until Bob told me that maybe I wasn't paying attention to the real meaning of Easter.

He suggested I read a story called An Easter Carol. Let's see what it says!

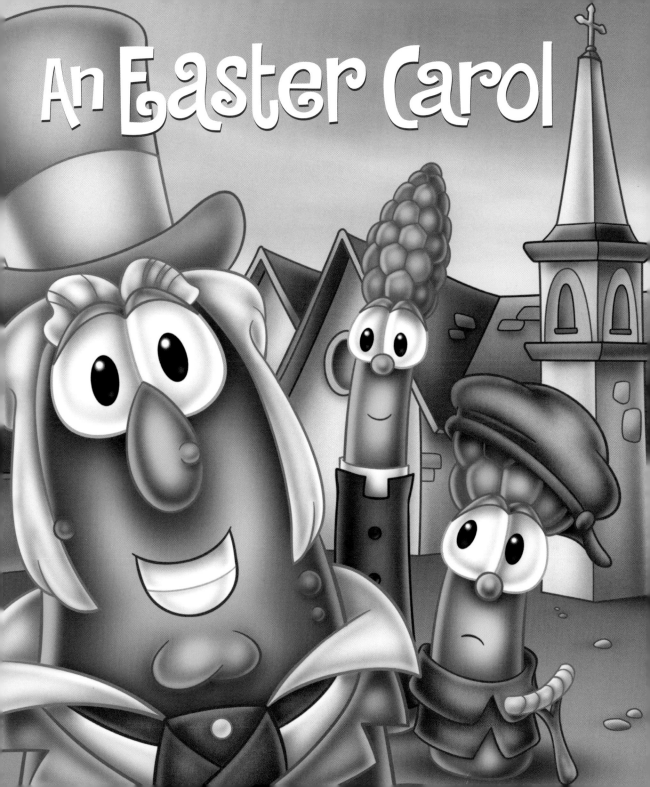

Bah! People should be buying more Easter eggs!

While Edmund and his dad prepared St. Bart's Church for Easter, Ebenezer Nezzer was hard at work making Easter eggs in his factory.

"Ah ... the satisfying fatigue of productivity!" Ebenezer chuckled.

Everyone begged Ebenezer to close the factory for Easter, but Ebenezer had another plan. He was going to destroy St. Bart's and build a place called Easter Land!

At midnight on Easter Eve, Ebenezer was fast asleep. WHACK!

Suddenly, he was awakened by a tiny angel named Hope.

Hope whisked him away and, before he knew what happened, Ebenezer was flying through the air towards St. Bart's Church.

Inside, he saw a little boy sitting next to his grandmother.

"That's you!" said Hope. "This is Easter past."

Before they left the church, Ebenezer saw the sunlight pouring through a stained-glass window that showed the birth of Jesus.

He just
needs
to find
out what
Easter is
really all
about.

A few minutes later, Ebenezer was watching himself as a grown up!

"This is Easter present," said Hope.

They saw little Edmund, who was very sick. "Mr. Nezzer isn't a bad man," Edmund told his father, "he just doesn't have something that we all have—the thing that lets us celebrate Easter all year long."

Ebenezer still didn't understand.

Back at St. Bart's Church, Hope tried
one more time to explain the true meaning
of Easter. She used the stained-glass
windows to show Ebenezer the
story of Jesus as she sang:
"A baby was born on a dark,
starry night. Some
followed the
star to see
the great
sight! The
years hurried by,
and the boy, now
a man, could make
the blind see with the
touch of his hand."

"He hated injustice — he taught what was right. He said, 'I'm the Way and the Truth and the Light.'

"His friends soon believed that he was the one, the Savior, Messiah; in fact, God's own Son.

"But others, they doubted, they did not agree. So they took him, they tried him; he died on a tree.

"There is nothing to fear, nothing, heaven knows. He died for us to give us life, and to give us hope, he rose."

CRASH!

Hope's song came to a crashing end as the wrecking ball smashed through the first window of the church! Ebenezer woke from his sleep.

Death will never be the end, if you just believe!

"Wait!" Ebenezer yelled as he ran down the street, through the door, and up the aisle of St. Bart's Church. "I was wrong! Easter isn't about plastic eggs. It's all about hope that this life isn't all there is!"

Edmund smiled up at Mr. Nezzer, who promised to use the money he saved for Easter Land to help make him well. **End**

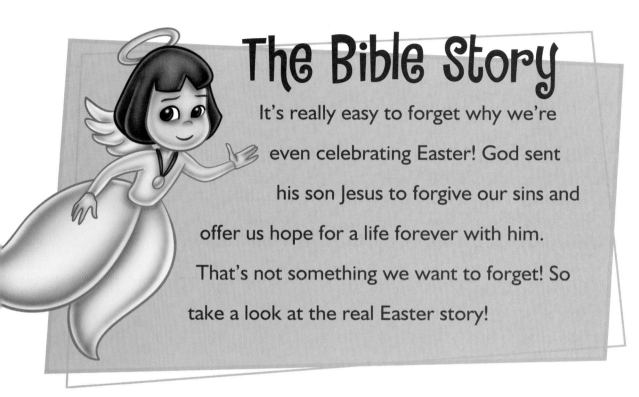

The Bible Story

It's really easy to forget why we're even celebrating Easter! God sent his son Jesus to forgive our sins and offer us hope for a life forever with him. That's not something we want to forget! So take a look at the real Easter story!

Jesus Is Risen

selections from Luke 24:1-10

It was very early in the morning on the first day of the week. The women took the spices they had prepared. Then they went to the tomb. They found the stone rolled away from it. When they entered the tomb, they did not find the body of the Lord Jesus.

They were wondering about this. Suddenly two men in clothes as bright as lightning stood beside them. The women were terrified [and] bowed down with their faces to the ground. Then the men said to them, "Why do you look for the living among the dead? Jesus is not here! He has risen! Remember how he told you he would rise. It was while he was still with you in Galilee. He said, 'The Son of Man must be handed over to sinful people. He must be nailed to a cross. On the third day he will rise from the dead.'" Then the women remembered Jesus' words. They came back from the tomb.

Why do you look for the living among the dead? Jesus is not here! He has risen!

They told all these things to the Eleven and to all the others. Mary Magdalene, Joanna, Mary the mother of James, and the others with them were the ones who told the apostles.

Wow.

It's good to be reminded of what's really important. I mean, I like my yellow-and-pink-spotted malted milk balls, my fuzzy, yellow, squeaky chicks, and my white, furry Easter rabbit. But they don't mean near as much to me as Jesus! Jesus is what Easter is all about.

So, just remember, it's okay to enjoy the plastic eggs and baskets. I hope you remember the real reason we celebrate Easter every year, too. In fact, Easter is one of the reasons we know that ...

God made you special and he loves you very much!

God loved the world so much that he gave his one and only son. Anyone who believes in him will not die but will have eternal life. — John 3:16

Well hello there!

Bob and I just bought new hats. Bob got a baseball cap, but I wanted something adventurous, like a fedora. Even the name sounds daring!

On our way home the Mushroom brothers knocked our hats right off our heads, and took them! As we were plotting our revenge, Princess Petunia saw us and encouraged us to read Minnesota Cuke. She said it might help us figure out what to do.

You'll never get away with this, Rattan!

Splat! Minnesota Cuke plunged into the powdery snowball as he grasped the golden carrot nose from the Indomitable Snowman of the North.

"Aha! Finders keepers!" shouted Professor Rattan as he snatched the treasure away. Rattan had ruined everything ... again.

LATER THAT DAY ...

"Rattan's just a bully, Minnesota," Marten said, trying to console Minnesota over the phone. "I need to find Samson's hairbrush," Minnesota replied. "Then I will have all

the power
and Rattan
can never bully
me again," he said
as he grabbed his
hat. "I'm going out
for ice cream!"

A LITTLE LATER ...

Minnesota smiled
at the beautiful
rhubarb at Malta Malts.
"Hello, Julia. I'm looking
for Samson's hairbrush."

"Don't, Minnesota. It's too dangerous,"
Julia pleaded.

But with a tip of his fedora and wink of
his eye, she gave him the address.

Minnesota Cuke, I always knew that someday you'd come walkin' through my door.

LATER STILL ...

Minnesota Cuke headed deep into the catacombs and shined his flashlight on the cave drawings. "It's the story of Samson. Wow! What a guy!" Minnesota said, looking at the muscular Peach wrestling a lion.

He carefully crossed a rickety bridge that led to a pedestal holding the hairbrush.

"Congratulations, Mr. Cuke!" It was his archnemesis standing smugly at the other end of the bridge!

"Hand over the brush," Rattan ordered.

"Never! I have the power now!" Minnesota said.

But Rattan had captured Julia! "It's a simple trade, Minnesota. The brush for the beautiful girl!"

"Don't do it, Cuke!" Julia called.

Minnesota had no choice. He handed over the brush.

"We have to stop him! He's a bully! I've got to get even with him!" Minnesota shouted after Rattan disappeared.

Don't do it, Cuke!

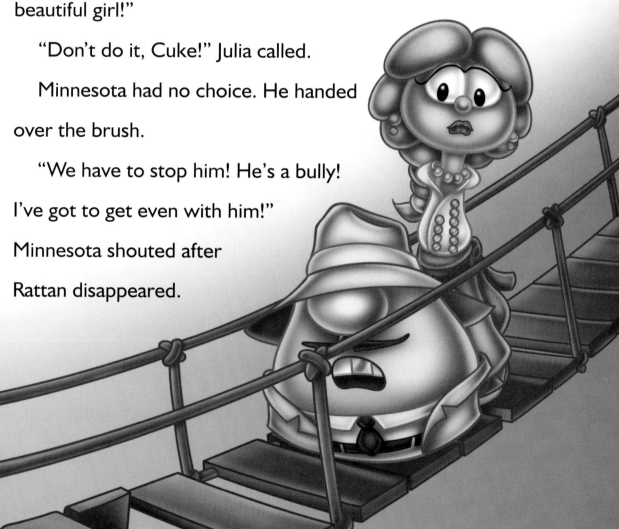

Stand back, all of you! I have a brush and I know how to use it!

"The Bible says we should love our enemies," Julia said. "We can't go around trying to get even all the time! That would leave the whole world in a mess!"

"I'm sorry, Julia," Minnesota said. "Being mean back to a bully just makes me a bully, too. But with that hairbrush, Rattan can rule the world!"

"The Bible says God gave Samson his power, not his hair or hairbrush," Julia said.

"I know what I have to do!" Minnesota said as he dashed off to catch up with Rattan.

MOMENTS LATER ...

"Stand back. I have a brush and I know how to use it!" Rattan ordered.

But Marten had called the police and

they arrived just in time for Rattan.

"Let him go, fellas!" Minnesota said. "God gives us the power to love everybody, even our enemies."

"No one has ever been kind to me before!" Rattan said. "I'm really sorry. Here's your hairbrush."

"Nah. You need it to cover that little bald spot you're getting," Minnesota replied as he fixed Rattan's hair.

"I think I'm gonna like being friends!" **End**

The Bible Story

Seeking revenge on our enemies isn't the answer. Look to God for strength and treat others with respect and kindness. Let's read what the Bible says about this ...

Wise Advice

selections from Romans 12:9-21

Love must be honest and true. Hate what is evil. Hold on to what is good. Love each other deeply. Honor others more than yourselves. Never let the fire in your heart go out. Keep it alive. Serve the Lord. When you hope, be joyful. When you suffer, be patient. When you pray, be faithful. Share with God's people who are in need. Welcome others into your homes. Bless those who hurt you. Bless them, and do not call down curses on them. Be joyful with those who are joyful. Be sad with those who are sad.

Agree with each other. Don't be proud. Be willing to be a friend of people who aren't considered important. Don't think that you are better than others. Don't pay back evil with evil. Be careful to do what everyone thinks is right. If possible, live in peace with everyone. Do that as much as you can.

My friends, don't try to get even. Leave room for God to show his anger. It is written, "I am the One who judges people. I will pay them back," (Deuteronomy 32:35) says the Lord. Do just the opposite. Scripture says, "If your enemies are hungry, give them food to eat. If they are thirsty, give them something to drink.

If possible, live in peace with everyone. Do that as much as you can.

By doing those things, you will pile up burning coals on their heads." (Proverbs 25:21, 22) Don't let evil overcome you. Overcome evil by doing good.

Let's talk about this.

Bob and I have been rethinking our strategy. We've decided that getting revenge on the Mushroom brothers isn't such a good idea after all. We're trying to remember that God wants us to love everyone—even the Mushroom brothers!

So Bob and I have decided to go hat shopping again. This time we're going to pick out hats FOR the Mushroom brothers. Maybe they've never had new hats of their own! Doesn't matter. We know that it's better to do what's right by trying to be kind to them, even if they are bullies. That's what God wants us to do.

Because ...
God made you special and he loves you very much!

219

Hi there!

Have you ever played that game where you toss rings over a pop bottle and win prizes? Well, I am the VeggieTales champion! That's right. I always win! The other day we were at the carnival and Bob wanted this purple plastic squirrel. But I tossed my ring first and I won it! V-I-C-T-O-R-Y!

Bob said it was time for an attitude check. He made me read the story of Lyle the Kindly Viking.

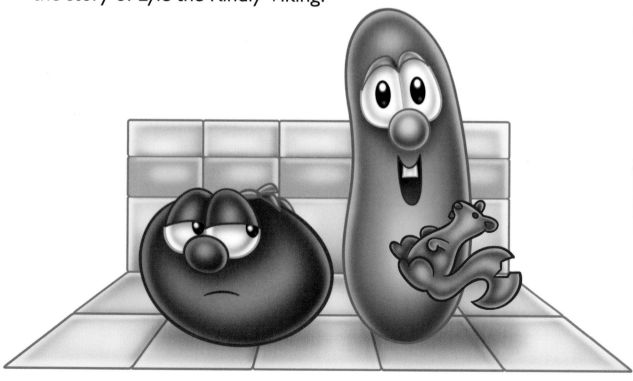

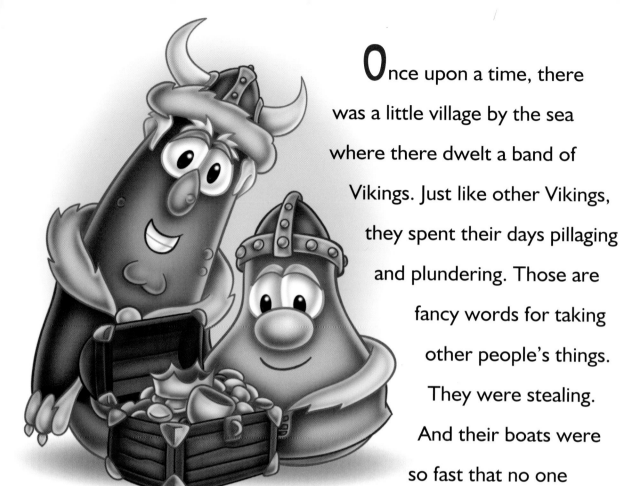

Once upon a time, there was a little village by the sea where there dwelt a band of Vikings. Just like other Vikings, they spent their days pillaging and plundering. Those are fancy words for taking other people's things. They were stealing. And their boats were so fast that no one could catch them so they could get away —every time.

But not all the Vikings were involved in this unfortunate practice. There was one Viking named Lyle who didn't like to go on the raids.

We never say please, or give stuff back!

In fact, when the other Vikings returned from their raids, Lyle would take the small bag of loot they gave him (along with some potholders that he made), and he would head out across the sea in his tiny boat.

When I share, I get my share of friends!

I'm telling you, that boy doesn't fit the Viking style.

The other Vikings didn't know where Lyle was going. So, Sven and Ottar decided to follow him and see.

What they saw was troubling, to say the least. Lyle was taking his bag of loot and returning it to the monastery they had raided the night before. Sven and Ottar knew if Olaf—the biggest, meanest Viking—found out, Lyle would be in BIG trouble. So they decided not to tell.

Then one day, Olaf and the

other Vikings were out in their big, fast boat. "Hey, isn't that Lyle over there?" Olaf asked as he looked through his binoculars.

Sven and Ottar tried to distract Olaf so he wouldn't see what Lyle was doing, but it was too late. Olaf knew what Lyle was up to and got very mad. "That little Viking is in BIG trouble," he yelled.

Look, the monks saved Lyle. I guess if we had shared, there'd be somebody to save us, too.

It didn't take long for the Vikings to catch Lyle in his little boat. But just as they caught him, a huge storm blew up. The waves were so big that all the Vikings were thrown into the sea.

"Hang on, Lyle. Help is on the way!" the monks yelled as they scrambled to save Lyle from the angry waters.

"What about my friends?" Lyle asked when he reached dry land.

"Well, they were mean to us," the monks replied.

"I'm pretty sure God wants us to help everybody, not just those who are nice."

"Oh, all right," the monks said. "We're monks; we should know that."

So, not only did the monks save Lyle, they saved all the Vikings that day—all because Lyle had made friends with them by sharing. **End**

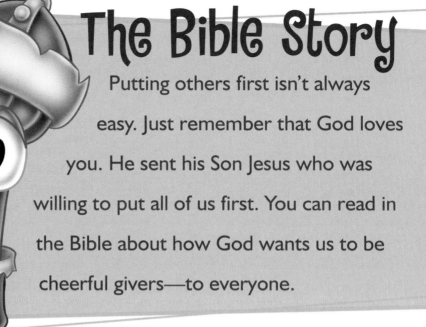

The Bible Story

Putting others first isn't always easy. Just remember that God loves you. He sent his Son Jesus who was willing to put all of us first. You can read in the Bible about how God wants us to be cheerful givers—to everyone.

A Cheerful Giver

selections from 2 Corinthians 9:7-9, 11-15

You should each give what you have decided in your heart to give. You shouldn't give if you don't want to. You shouldn't give because you are forced to. God loves a cheerful giver. And God is able to shower all kinds of blessings on you. In all things and at all times you will have everything you need. You will do more and more good works. It is written, "They have spread their gifts around to poor people. Their good works continue forever." (Psalm 112:9) You will be made rich in every way. Then you can always give freely. We will take your many gifts to the people who need them. And they will give thanks to God. Your gifts meet the needs of God's people. And that's not all. Your gifts also cause many people to thank God. You have shown yourselves to be worthy by what you have given. So people will praise God because you obey him. That proves that you really believe the good news about Christ. They will also praise God because you share freely with them and with everyone else.

> They will also praise God because you share freely with them and with everyone else.

Their hearts will be filled with longing for you when they pray for you. God has given you grace that is better than anything.

Let us give thanks to God for his gift. It is so great that no one can tell how wonderful it really is!

Attitude checked.

I really do like that plastic squirrel. And even more than the plastic squirrel, I liked winning. But I like Bob more than either of those things. So I gave the squirrel to Bob.

It's important to treat others fairly and to be kind, like Lyle. And you know what? It's really fun to share!

It's time for me to start putting others first, no matter what I'm doing. That way, everyone wins!

I hope you'll remember that God wants you to put others first, too.

After all ...
God made you special and he loves you very much!

None of you should look out just for your own good. You should also look out for the good of others.
— Philippians 2:4

Hi boys and girls!

Have you ever seen someone and thought, "Wow! They sure are different!" I have. In fact, there's this kid in my home economics class who likes to wear his oven mit on his head. The kids and I decided he was a little, um ... crazy!

After class, I bumped into Junior Asparagus and told him all about him. He told me to read a story about some gourds that were really different, too. I love stories ... so why not!

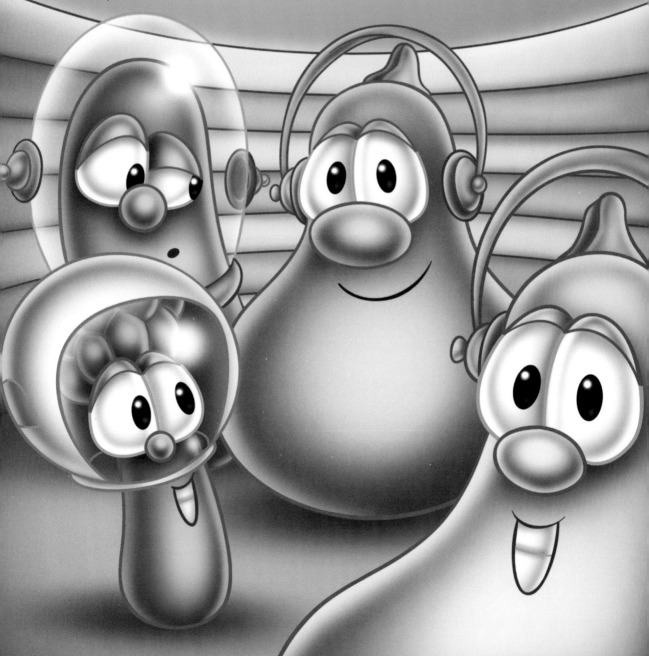

The Gourds Must Be Crazy

WHOOSH

went the elevator on the U.S.S. Applepies as Captain Bob stepped out on the control deck.

"Ah, Cap'n Bob!" said Scooter, the spaceship's engineer. "We've only five minutes till that popcorn meteor smashes us to bits!"

Everyone gasped. They were in big trouble.

"Is it caramel or cheese?" asked Larry. "That cheese stuff gets stuck to my tooth."

"Hey, maybe they can help!" Junior said, pointing to the gourds working by themselves.

The ship has no power! She's dead in the water! She's stuck!

"They're the 'new guys!' " Scooter said. "All they do is eat and sing. I think they're a wee bit crazy!"

"I'm Junior, and we've got a problem," he said to the new guys.

"I'm Jimmy."

"I'm Jerry. We're the new guys."

"I heard," Junior said. "Why do you guys sing and eat all the time?"

"Why don't you?" asked Jerry.

"I dunno!" said Junior. "Because it's weird ... uh, I mean different."

A popcorn ball meteor. The worst kind!

We're hungry. It's our metabolism.

"Sometimes differences can be good," said Jimmy Gourd. "In fact, I think I could eat a whole bus!"

"I think I could eat a whole spaceship!" said Jerry.

"I could eat a whole planet!" said Jimmy.

"A whole planet?" Junior had an idea. "How would you like to help save the ship?"

"Gosh," said Jimmy, that'd be swell!"

So Bob, Larry, Junior, and Scooter helped the Gourds into the only two escape pods on the ship.

"We've only got two minutes left!" said Bob. "I sure hope this works!"

The pods fired up and shot deep into space until PLOMPH!!! The pods hit the meteor!

We're all pretty different. Some are skinny, some are stout,

"Let's eat it!" the gourds shouted. And they ate and ate and ate and ATE!

Meanwhile, back on the ship, everyone was very nervous.

"Only ten seconds left!" said Bob. "I sure hope they were hungry! Five ... Four ... Three ... Two ... ONE!!!"

THUNK! Jimmy and Jerry knocked on the door!

"Boy, am I full!" said Jimmy.

"Mission accomplished. You saved the ship!" said Bob.

"Aw ... It was nothing!"

"Nothing?" said Scooter. "You consumed fourteen thousand metric tons o' popcorn, lads!"

"Well," said Jimmy, "maybe it's a little something."

"To think I wouldn't be your friend just because you guys are different!" said Scooter. "I'm glad you're my friends!"

"We are, too!" agreed a very full and happy Jimmy and Jerry. **End**

but the inside is the part that we're supposed to care about!

The Bible Story

Being different is okay! God made everyone different—and special—in their own way. Here's a story about a guy who was really different. But God had a special purpose for him, too.

The Conversion of Paul
selections from Acts 9:1-19

Saul continued to oppose the Lord's followers. On his journey, suddenly a light from heaven flashed around him. He fell to the ground. He heard a voice speak to him.

"Saul! Saul!" the voice said. "Why are you opposing me?"

"Who are you, Lord?" Saul asked.

"I am Jesus," he replied. "I am the one you are opposing. Now get up and go into the city. There you will be told what to do."

The men traveling with Saul stood there. They weren't able to speak. They had heard the sound. But they didn't see anyone. Saul got up from the ground. He opened his eyes, but he couldn't see. So they led him by the hand into [the city]. For three days he was blind. He didn't eat or drink anything.

In [the city] there was a believer named Ananias. The Lord called out to him in a vision. "Go to the house of Judas. Ask for a man named Saul. He is praying. "Go! I have chosen this man to work for me. He will carry my name to those who aren't Jews and to their kings. He will bring my name to the people of Israel."

Something like scales fell from Saul's eyes.

Ananias went to the house. He placed his hands on Saul [and said,] "Brother Saul, you saw the Lord Jesus on the road as you were coming here. He has sent me so that you will be able to see again. You will be filled with the Holy Spirit." Something like scales fell from Saul's eyes. And he could see again. He got up and was baptized.

Back to school!

I went back to my home economics class and decided to clear up my differences with the new kid! I went over and introduced myself, and I discovered he was a lot of fun! He taught me a really great recipe for toast, and we had a great time. I also discovered that it's kind of fun to wear an oven mit on my head. After all, I don't have any hands to put it on!

Isn't it wonderful that God made everyone different? It sure does make things interesting—and a lot more fun, too!

Remember ...
God made you special and he loves you very much!

Christ has accepted you. So accept one another in order to bring praise to God.
— Romans 15:17

Hello boys and girls!

I have a new hobby. Gardening! Nothing lifts the spirits like a little dabbling in the horticultural arts. And I'm really good at it, too. I'm going to enter my dandelion patch in the Lawn and Garden show. My neighbor, Mrs. Stephenson, is entering the contest, too. But Percy Pea told me that she has poison ivy in her flower bed.

I was just on my way to tell the judges about that when Bob stopped me. He said he had a story I'd better listen to before I tell anybody what I'd heard.

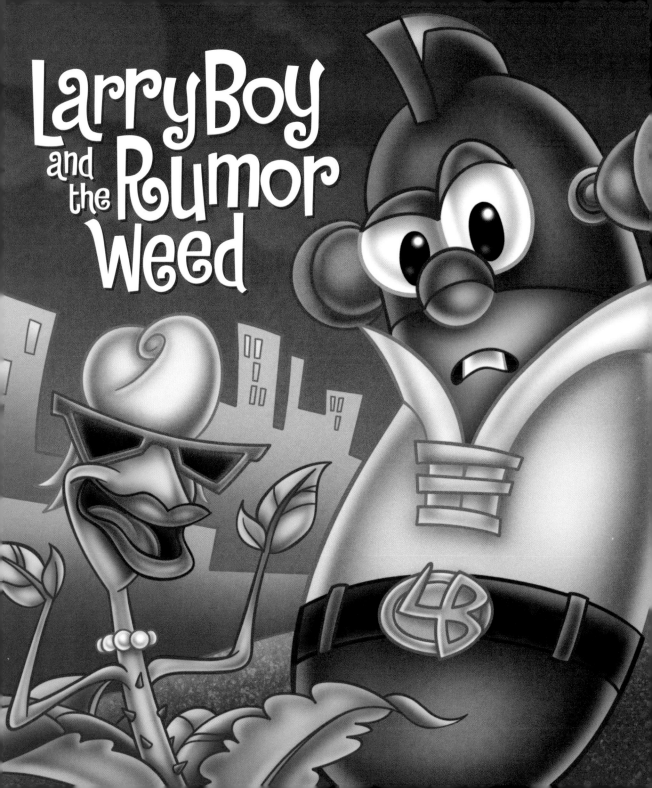

T hank you so much for having me!" Alfred the butler said as he finished his Career Day speech at the Veggie Valley Grade School. "I'd love to stay longer but I'm very tired. I'd better go home and 'recharge my batteries!'"

LATER THAT DAY ...

"Did you hear what Mr. Alfred said?" Junior asked Laura as they walked home from school.

"Yeah," Laura replied, "he said he had to go home and recharge his batteries. I think Mr. Alfred IS ... A ... ROBOT."

Suddenly a strange voice came out of nowhere. "What was that you said?"

"Who said that?" Laura asked as she looked down and saw ... a TALKING WEED.

"C'mon, tell me what it is you're keeping to yourselves," the weed continued. "Didn't your parents ever teach you to share?"

"Well, we learned something about Mr. Alfred today," Junior explained. "We think he's ... a robot!"

I'm a talking weed. You're a talking carrot. Your point was?

I'm a Rumor Weed! A tiny little story is all I need.

MOMENTS LATER ...

The weed showed up in Percy Pea's yard. She told Percy that Mr. Alfred was a dangerous robot. Soon, the Rumor Weed was introducing herself all over Bumblyburg.

"So what is a rumor?" Mr. Nezzer asked.

"A rumor starts with a story," the weed explained. "Maybe it's true, maybe not. But once you repeat it, it's hard to defeat it. Now look at the mess that you've got!"

It was true, every time someone in the city repeated the rumor, the weed got bigger. Soon, weeds were popping up all over the city. They were feeding on the story that Junior and Laura had started.

The weed was growing powerful roots capable of breaking sidewalks and even going through walls. If something wasn't done about this terrible Rumor Weed, the city would be ruined!

There was only one thing to do. The mayor picked up the phone and called ... LarryBoy!

I am that hero!

249

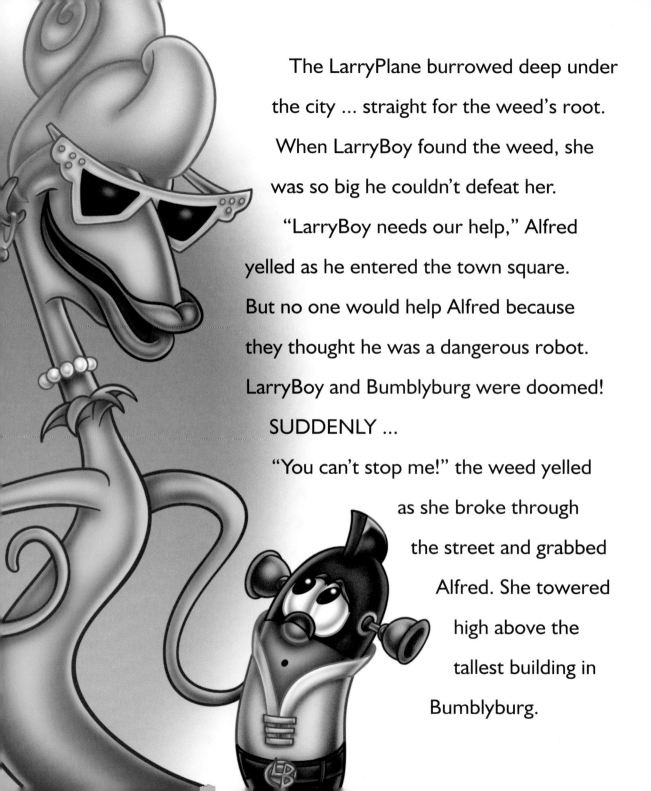

The LarryPlane burrowed deep under the city ... straight for the weed's root. When LarryBoy found the weed, she was so big he couldn't defeat her.

"LarryBoy needs our help," Alfred yelled as he entered the town square. But no one would help Alfred because they thought he was a dangerous robot. LarryBoy and Bumblyburg were doomed! SUDDENLY ...

"You can't stop me!" the weed yelled as she broke through the street and grabbed Alfred. She towered high above the tallest building in Bumblyburg.

MEANWHILE ...

On the street, Junior's dad asked the kids what happened.

"Well, we heard Mr. Alfred say that he needed to recharge his batteries," Laura explained. "We thought he was a robot."

"Mr. Alfred isn't a robot," Dad Asparagus said. "He's a very nice man."

As he said those nice words, the weed sprouted blooms.

Soon, the whole town began saying nice words about Alfred, and the Rumor Weed turned into a beautiful flower.

"God doesn't want us to spread words that hurt, he wants us to spread nice words." End

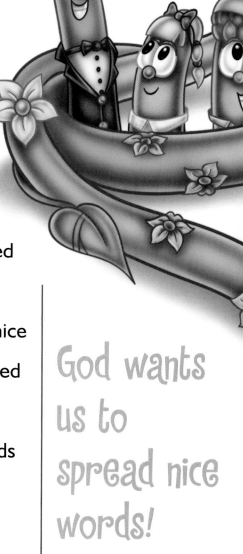

God wants us to spread nice words!

The Bible Story

The Rumor Weed is much more dangerous than a real weed in the garden. I couldn't even defeat it by attacking the roots! The only way to beat the Rumor Weed was by spreading nice words. Here's a great Bible passage about this ...

New Life ... New Ways
selections from Colossians 3:8-17

But now here are the kinds of things you must get rid of. You must put away anger, rage, hate and lies. Let no dirty words come out of your mouths. Don't lie to each other. You have gotten rid of your old way of life and its habits. You have started living a new life. It is being made new so that what you know has the

Creator's likeness … There is no slave or free person. But Christ is everything. And he is in everything.

You are God's chosen people. You are holy and dearly loved. So put on tender mercy and kindness as if they were your clothes. Don't be proud. Be gentle and patient. Put up with each other. Forgive the things you are holding against one another. Forgive, just as the Lord forgave you. And over all of those good things put on love. Love holds them all together perfectly as if they were one.

Don't lie to each other.

Let the peace that Christ gives rule in your hearts. As parts of one body, you were appointed to live in peace. And be thankful. Let Christ's word live in you like a rich treasure. Teach and correct each other wisely. Sing psalms, hymns and spiritual songs. Sing with thanks in your hearts to God. Do everything you say or do in the name of the Lord Jesus. Always give thanks to God the Father through Christ.

OK...

So Bob was right. Not even the coveted Bumblyburg Lawn and Garden trophy is worth spreading a rumor about my neighbor, Mrs. Stephenson. Even if she really has poison ivy in her garden, the judges aren't going to hear it from me. They'll probably figure that out for themselves.

God doesn't want us to say mean or bad things about each other. God wants us to spread only nice words.

Remember...
God made you special and he loves you very much!

254

Those who lead honest people down an evil path will fall into their own trap.

— Proverbs 28:10

More Favorites from Big Idea Books!

0-310-70466-9

0-310-70623-8

0-310-70540-1

0-310-70539-8

0-310-70538-X

0-310-70541-X

0-310-70784-6

0-310-70783-8

0-310-70781-1

0-310-70467-7

0-310-70702-1

ZONDERk!dz

ZONDERVAN.com/
AUTHORTRACKER
follow your favorite authors

We want to hear from you!

Please send your comments about this book to us in care of
zreview@zondervan.com. Thank you.

Grand Rapids, MI 49530
www.zonderkidz.com